Waiting for a Hunter's Moon

by Simon Smith

Copyright © Simon Smith

All rights reserved.

Print ISBN 978-1-8382805-9-8

The right of Simon Smith to be identified as the author of this work has been asserted by him in accordance with the Copyright Designs and Patents Act 1988

No part of this publication may be reproduced, stored in a retrieval system, or transmitted in any form or by any means without the prior permission in writing of the publisher. Nor be otherwise circulated in any form or binding or cover other than that in which it is published and without a similar condition being imposed on the subsequent purchaser.

All characters and events in this publication, other than those clearly in the public domain, are fictitious and any resemblance to real persons, living or dead, is purely coincidental.

Published by

Llyfrau Cambria Books, Wales, United Kingdom.

Cambria Books is a division of

Cambria Publishing Ltd.

Discover our other books at: www.cambriabooks.co.uk

For Rachel and Elle
*-by my side at all times,
through all seasons.*

Also by Simon Smith:

Running with the Tide, (Medlar Press, 2013)

CONTENTS

I – At the Year's Opening ... 2
    New Year ... 3
    Frost ... 6
    Filling in the … ... 7
    Wait, stars ... 17

II – The Growing Year ... 18
    Notes from the Margins ... 19
    Just ... 27
    Weather-eye ... 28
        I - Storm ... 28
        II – Afterward ... 32
    Keeping Faith ... 33
    Lost and Found ... 40
    Lugman ... 43

III – Year's Fullness ... 44
    Cry Havoc! ... 45
    Foreigners ... 50
    Day tickets and Daydreams ... 54
    The Button-Jar ... 58
    The Sunbird ... 69
    Guillemot ... 79
    Turning on the Dark ... 80

IV – Year's Turning ... 88
    Waiting for a Hunter's Moon ... 89
    The Derelicts ... 90
    Last Look ... 101
    Genus: Piscator ... 108

Equinoctial	110
This Sympathetic Magic	119
V – At the Year's Closing	126
At This Time of the Rolling Year	127
Breakwater	132
A Trillion Blooms	139
Editorials	140

At the Shoreline,

                this tabula rasa.

Would it bear me if my course were to bend
down toward the waterline and away around the empty bay?

Perhaps not. Perhaps it's nothing more than a flimsy vellum sheet
waiting to be weighted down before the wind flusters it away.
Still, I'll walk the tilt and lift of those uncharted topographies
and know for myself the true meaning of *terra incognita*.

If there's any truth in what they say, if no man is an island, then let
him settle instead for this: the empty welcome of shorelines
where days run aground on their own end; where history rolls in.

I – At the Year's Opening

New Year

We have arrived. Or at least, we feel we have arrived.

New Year.

For twelve months we have seemed to plough our way toward this space in the calendar and yet, when we find ourselves at that point upon which we have focused for so long, we are left standing as émigrés on a far shore, our heads abundant with thoughts and dreams and our pockets turned out and empty.

Once again, the clock has zeroed and we have no time under our belts at all, only twelve more empty months to fill, or *a twelvemonth* as my grandfather used to call it, lending an antique substance to the intangible, a satisfying quantity and gravitas that allows it to be rightfully measured alongside a *fathom* or a *hundredweight*.

So, rather than an arrival, we have perhaps come to something we would be better to describe as a 'negotiated newness', a time of great loss but, perhaps, of even greater truth. The "clammy cells" of autumn have long since been ransacked and now lie stripped and left exposed to the elements. Whatever remains is now up for grabs as this new year has yet to begin pencilling in its first outlines, meaning that anyone can come and begin to give, or take, whatever definition they desire.

Everything has a sharpness, a no-frills air of frugality about it. Pavements bleached pale by road salt are left with the quality of the very cheapest cuts of meat – sparse, a utilitarian white flash of bone showing through the thin flesh. Even the air carries a razored quality, like a favourite knife stropped and re-stropped to a wafer-thin tolerance that threatens to snap with every lancing cut it makes through my clothing.

Everywhere, the landscape is brittle, cowering into its own fragility. Freezing air flares across exposed skin, burning fast and deep, and everywhere I step the chiming grass stems and iced sand craze into craquelure patterns underfoot. Already, the verges of the world are strewn with hours that have seized up, refused to budge, and now lie knackered and abandoned in their own chilly indifference.

Just this afternoon the walk home from work brought me past the river where it sat in a schizophrenic limbo. The trickle of water slid up against the shallow, weeded, ice-bound margins that had just started to steam in the feeble remnants of the limp afternoon sunlight; all three stages of water lay alongside each other to tell the story of an element that was unsure in which state it wished to exist.

But now evening comes on.

Even as it begins to fail in this final pre-dark period, the light dangles lifelessly, a blanket made up of more holes than fabric, slightly shading the town but not yet enough to bring about total darkness, letting in a chill at the neck or the feet at the first available opportunity. Even the glow of the first stars seems cold and unmoving, having lost any warmth on its journey of decades, centuries, millennia, to reach here, an obsolete image from something long dead. Not many would venture out on such an evening.

But for all its early brittleness this is definitely a beginning, even though it may not at first be evident. The world's eternal turning has swung into motion once again.

And now they come as if by instinct, following their sidereal circuits that have always led them here, to these places at these times, sensing perhaps that hard ground does not mean lifeless ground. Where many see emptiness, they look deeper, seeing a wide world uncluttered; a sea or river that seems to have been erased, replaced by the shine of stars and a rind of moonlight left to wither on a surface uncreased by swell or wind or wave, doubling the open spaces so that everything bumbles through it and into it like a lost echo. The stilled machinery of frozen water still harbours a faint memory of movement.

And so they continue, these resurrection men and women; plumbing the quiet depths with their floats, setting their rod tips into the wind and current, they strain, watch, wait to adjust to the gentle turn of the year's first tide, the slow, shy flow of the stream.

They tilt their heads back once more to take in the stars, or what, at least, appear to be the stars, their light still burning in defiance against a death long since past.

In the silence the float dibs; the rod tip trembles; the heart quickens.

There is life yet.

Frost

Here, on the estuary's forgotten shore,
away from the road's tarmac gravity,
the dark begins to pool early against
high boulder banks and the dune's downslope.

Another swarm of dreams is scattering south.
With a luthier's ear for resonance
and absences, the river channels out
its own meandering chamber-course.

Snow stillness; snow silence. And yet no snow:
"Too cold for it". Deep cold, more than enough
to snuff the stars into a charred blackness
and scorch this great dark bore hole to the moon.

Everything is drawn of its ghosts
and now the frost begins to populate
this void, creeping from every crack and crevice,
extrapolating brittle feathered forms
so exact
        humerus to radius
so intricate
              radius to ulna;
each shiny new angle geared for flight
yet still grounded come first light of morning.

Filling in the ...

The streamers seem barely to have stopped falling, the chime of bells quit ringing out in our ears, and already we are almost a week into this New Year. Well, at least, it is according to the Gregorian system of marking time.

My life, unfortunately, never seems to follow quite such a straightforward path, so constantly is it caught in the crosscurrents of many other systems. We are a few months from the end of the financial year, a third of the way into the academic year, the liturgical year has only barely begun, and the first new shoots of spring are as yet a distant thought. Sometimes it is difficult to decide whether I am coming or going or merely bobbing about helplessly somewhere in the middle.

So, what now?

Some will spend their time looking back, picking over the bones of what has passed, but I won't be amongst their number. I am usually hugely enthusiastic about Christmas but even I, after a slightly unpleasant year, am glad to leave it behind for once. The season of Christmas will soon be over anyway; in a strangely apt kind of symbolism a large fir, downed by recent winds, lies half-leaning across the mountain path I'm walking as it turns to face back in toward the Afan Valley. The valley itself is almost as hollow as this post-season period. I have read that it is the disease Phytophtora Ramorum or, to give it its tabloid moniker, 'Sudden Oak Death', that is responsible for the emptiness of the hills. Large swathes of larches have been infected, the disease proliferating in the milder, wet conditions caused by our prevailing south-westerly winds, meaning that they have had to be felled, stripped and stacked, and now lie piled up in eerie stacks like some great wooden elephant graveyard.

The departure of Christmas will pave the way for the less than inspirational sounding Ordinary Time, which will itself be followed by the austerities of Lent, so perhaps it's best not to think too far ahead for solace either.

There will be lots of timid beginnings now – notebooks folded along spines and marked with *'Dear Diary'*; brand new pairs of trainers and jogging kit will be unwrapped and slipped on, and perhaps for the first time, new packets of cigarettes will not be bought to replace those just smoked. A few of these will last and become something more permanent, and some will simply end just as quickly as they began, the training kit tossed to the back of the wardrobe or the pages ripped from the notebooks.

Others, less concerned with resolutions perhaps, having enjoyed their life to the full over the last year, will simply set their faces into whatever is to come and wait in an excited anticipation of the unknown, treating it as one big, shiny new fresh start.

Many others, like me, won't have a clue which way to turn, so it will simply be a case of taking it one step at a time.

Next comes Epiphany with its thoughts of the Adoration of the Magi. Imagine the distance they must have wandered; imagine the terrain they must have had to negotiate to reach their destination. Maybe not so bad though, when you carry with you the utter certainty that you need only follow the light of one star to complete your journey.

There was not just one, but a sky full of bright stars draped over my head last night, yet no such certainty for me as I packed the car. Momentarily they would disappear behind plumes of my own breath and drifting banks of thickening cloud, but then there they were again, simply hanging there in the sky's freezing clarity, neither they nor I seeming to have any kind of direction about us. Why do I do it? It was clearly a night for warm memories and hot tea and yet, against all better judgement, I had no choice but to go. I had been away from the water for a couple of weeks and maybe the codling would be feeding; maybe I'd be able to pick up a few whiting.

Maybe there would be nothing.

*

Parking the car, I began to unpack the box and the rods. In the short time it had taken to drive to the beach the sky had closed in. Even the car still wore its mantle of frost as though unsure whether I would be staying or turning back for home. But I was committed now. Here was a gap in the night that could only be filled by the sound of groundswell, the ping of line running through the rod rings. I pulled on my boots, shouldered the rod sling, grabbed the bucket and began to trudge the road that would lead me to the breakwater.

After only a few steps the first flakes of snow finally began to fall.

The sky that had been skulking about for the previous ten minutes had at last been embarrassed into action as though found out as a ditherer, and from such unpromising beginnings the wind found its sting, the flurry strengthened and suddenly everything was whiteout, finally lending at least a little credence to the sensationalist tabloid headlines that had bellowed 'WORST WINTER IN **100** YEARS' and 'FIVE MONTHS OF SNOW MISERY ON THE WAY' from their front pages over the last two months.

High tide was only an hour away and so, more out of necessity than judgement, instead of heading right toward the breakwater I could no longer see, I turned left. This path, I figured, would take me to the estuary where I could tuck myself behind the dunes, setting up my large umbrella out of the worst of the wind and snow.

Already the flurry was starting to lay a powdery crust from which my feet had started to take crunching bites. Looking back over my own tracks, they were already smudging into a fuzzy obscurity, the snow falling away from my feet mingling with the fresh falling powder that, together, did their best to erase my presence from the scene, leaving not so much something that could be described as footprints, but indefinable holes or gaps where the snow had been disturbed.

Strangely, far from being a dead loss, I often find that times like these are the best way of discovering anything new – new paths, new directions, new fishing spots – to allow myself to simply wander, blown about by luck and circumstance like a grain of sand until I fetch up against a place that stops me in my tracks. For the present, it's often better to live in the first draft with all its sketchy outlines, and let the technicalities come later when there's more information to play with. At the beginning though, all the new experiences should just be allowed to accrete slowly, the way a dune is formed, building and accumulating and giving life to these new places along fishing's vast songlines in the process.

Despite my pioneer outlook, I soon realised that I wouldn't be the one to lay down this track. Coming down into the lee of the dune, the sand here hadn't quite been covered in so much snow, leaving exposed an old bait packet and a few loops of monofilament line so sun-bleached that they could have been laid here six months or six years ago, uncovered now by the recent winds. But then, even those who walked out the animist songlines of the Antipodes never laid down anything that could be seen as final, preferring instead to sing their own version of the song loosely based around the verses left lying around the landscape for them. Maybe I had stumbled across a rickety old verse of this one, waiting for someone to just come along and sharpen it up, improving it with their own fortunes.

There were still blanks enough ahead of me though, as there are in front of any angler, the first of which lay dark and questioning immediately in front of me. The question might be phrased slightly differently, whether it be the slow coursing of the stream through the countryside, the endlessly deep ponds and lakes of literature and lore that have burrowed in to outplot and outwait mankind, or the tide that fails to make up its mind twice a day. The effect is always the same though. In such a state of unknowing the imagination begins to compensate, sketching in some of the details. Perhaps there's an undercut hole in the bank beneath your feet and, conjured up to occupy it, a fat chub or a scarred old pike waiting for an easy meal to wash down on the current. In the never-resolved jigsaw of the summer surf was that a bass, or perhaps a mullet? Or was it just weed?

Then to the cast. Near bank or far bank? Slow sink or medium sink? Overhead thump to thirty yards or pendulum cast to a hundred and thirty? And what lies in all that untouched water in between the two?

Perhaps the secret is solved, the blank filled in and the cast results in a take. In comes the fish, further, further still until, with a sickening twang, the line parts and leaves the angler with only a tall tale and a small piece of punctuation representing that one big question that will forever remain uresolved, and why not? Life's no fun when you have all the answers.

Sometimes, the line between memory and imagination becomes so blurred we forget which are the lived moments and which are the imaginings. As a boy, I spent hours roaming the land around the local lake formed by an inactive dock once used by the local steelworks. A true edgeland, areas of grass and shrub were punctuated by rubble patches and small piles of scrap metal – paradise for a young boy. Day after day of exploration and adventures to make any Health and Safety executive break into a sweat were lived, then logged away. Only years later, when I asked my father, a steelworker, about some of the things I remembered, were any of these experiences called into question.

First up was the house at the end of Dock Road. Dock Road was the name of the track that ran from the town centre down to the river bridge near the street where I grew up, but never was it an actual road or street. Yet I remember clearly wandering further than usual one day, then stumbling across the remains of an end-of-terrace house. Like one of those black and white images of a blitzed city in the Second World War, or some kind of gigantic doll's house, I could see both floors and even some of the attic space where the side wall had collapsed away, though not enough to remove the sign at the top that read DOCK ROAD. As I looked over it I imagined the invented lives of dockers and harbourmasters lived within those walls, and the now absent walls of others in the terrace. When I recounted these details to my father, he looked at me blankly, shook his head and told me that he had never heard of a Dock Road in his life.

Nor had he heard of the fish pit, the next memory I told him about.

Clear as day, a sunny day in fact, I was bumbling about my stamping grounds when I nearly stumbled into a sunlit pit around a hundred feet deep. With nothing to mark it out, and surrounded by grass and bramble, the pit couldn't be seen unless you were standing over it and staring down, as I was, looking into it as it descended to a pool, the surface of which was around twenty feet across. However, it was not the pit itself that held my attention, but what was swimming around in it.

Bright sunlight streamed down upon the surface of the pool which must, somehow, have been fed by some subterranean tunnel, allowing four or five huge fish to enter, cruising around in the sunlight. With hindsight, I imagine that they were probably mullet, but as I hadn't yet begun my fishing career, I had no idea what they were; I could only gawp on as they languidly wound S and unwound 2 through that bright patch of water.

Again my father denied all knowledge of any such pit, but even today, when I watch the summer mullet shoals winding upriver with the tide or the bass silhouetted against the breakwater's rocks, I think of that pit and those fabulous fish I never managed to wet a line for. To this day I still don't know whether or not I imagined these things, but I've happily come to settle on the idea that I'll never know, that they're always going to exist somewhere between fantasy and reminiscence, much like many of the best memories that life decides to leave us with.

*

The weather continued to close in, so I found an accessible spot to get the brolly up and the lantern lit, throwing the area behind its reach even further into shadow. The small hooks were baited with ragworms, prawns and mussels and quickly flung out into the dark before I retreated back to my seat, into a vacuum of silence and snow.

Gently, the spackling of snow on the umbrella settled into a steady rhythm and became the cadence of rain on a crusty old tarpaulin as I remembered myself back in the den I built with my friend a few hundred yards upstream over twenty-five years before. We beat the little hollow into the jungle of vegetation with sticks, dragging into its green cupola an old sofa we found, making it rainproof with that length of old tarpaulin, and we were everything we had ever dreamed we might be – princes, fugitives, men at ease with the great wide world into which we'd carved our own little cosy nook away from parents and homework and the thought of growing up. For the summer days that the den was in our lives we were Lost Boys.

Of course, we soon came to realise that nothing ever lasts, arriving one morning to find that a passer-by, the local homeless man most likely, had found it in the night as Ratty and Moley had stumbled across Mr. Badger's front door, and had bedded down for the night, leaving behind a gift of empty cider bottles and worn-down cigarette butts.

I had an early taste then of what acquaintances would later describe as the feeling when their house had been burgled – that sense of defilement that forever tarnished a place, taking away the sense of homely belonging for the owner. We went back once or twice after that, but the end of the summer holidays saw its complete abandonment. Soon after, the unbroken spine of dunes that formed our scrubby outpost of the town began to take the weight of development as house after red-bricked house was loaded upon the place where it had been, just as the progressive cares of life were placed on ours – education, jobs, families, all of which led me half a mile and a quarter-century back downstream to a cramped spot under an umbrella and the ceaseless tapping of snow reminding me that, even after all that time, I hadn't really come so far after all.

Nibbles weren't long in arriving, though they didn't warrant any action as there were only small fish out there pecking at the bait, too small to even hook themselves easily. I sat back further onto my seat, occasionally glancing up at the rod tips, but more often watching the still falling flakes accumulate upon the sand and the rocks around me, piling up softly on top of the reels, the rod rings, hearing its continual patter against the umbrella's fabric so that I was put in mind of the seventeenth century Japanese haiku poet Matsuo Basho's poem:

> *First snow*
> *falling*
> *on the half-finished bridge.*

Where would it eventually lead to, that bridge? Was it ever completed? I wondered if he ever gave in to that childish little voice inside all of us that would surely have urged him to take a step out onto that half-finished bridge, just one step, and look down over the edge. Bridges would have been important to a man like Basho, always on the go, journeying on foot around Japan's Edo Five Routes, coming to observe and know and love the changing of seasons and the progressions of life and death around him. For him, much of the joy of walking was the aloneness on a journey, the getting away from the bustle of life and the growing band of admirers that had begun to recognise his poetry. Even the dream written about in his last recorded poem is a wandering one, allowing his imagination to roam out across the landscape as he himself physically began to fail:

> ...*only my dreams will wander*
> *these desolate moors.*

Ah, hopefully there would be no failure for me though - there was a proper bite. And another. My fingers were freezing winding the rig in, but mercifully, it didn't take long before the fish emerged from the water – a dab that must have weighed all of two ounces.

This was it? This was all I was going to get? I began to make an effort to work the whole thing out: ten pounds on bait; a couple of pounds on petrol to get me there and back home again; not to mention the minor fortune spent on tackle. Then, of course, there were the adversities of the weather. I put up with all of this and all I was going to get out of it was one single, solitary dab that barely covered the palm of my (shrivelled, very cold) hand and was almost as transparent as a sheet of tracing paper.

But then, I wondered if it can it ever be so simply balanced like this? Does

[B]ait + [T]ime fished = [S]uccessful angling?

On the other hand, perhaps

[E]nthusiasm ^{2} x [T]ime fished + [Fi]sh caught = [H]appiness

Or even

$\sqrt{}$[S]atisfaction = [T]ime fished x [F]ish caught

The thought that angling could be reduced down to some

simple equation began to depress me, and I was never much good at Maths anyway, so I plopped the fish back and retreated to the shelter to try to restore some circulation to my withering digits with a warming cup of tea.

Suitably revived, I began to give that little fish a bit more credit. First, it managed to hold its own in all the tide and weed, and then it managed to find my bait and, somehow, muster enough energy to tug on the line enough for me to see the bite. Not bad at all.

So how did I measure up, the great judge and jury over all things piscatorial? Going back nearly two thousand years, another poet, the Greco-Roman Oppian, had very clear views as to what made a good angler, laying down his ideas in no uncertain terms in his great fishing poem *Halieutica*. Let's see:

"First of all the fisher should have body and limbs both swift and strong".

Okay, admittedly I'm not maybe as quick or as fit as I was ten years ago, but I like watching a bit of rugby.

"Cunning of wit, too, and wise should the fisher be since many and various are the devices that fishes contrive".

I've been called many things in my life but I can't remember wise being amongst them. Cunning? I'm probably the only man on the planet that has as little common sense as this.

Okay, there's got to be something in my favour here. What's the next thing?

"Daring also should he be and dauntless..."

Well, there was that time that I filled my flask with coffee rather than tea.

"He must not love satiety of sleep, but must be keen of sight, wakeful of heart and open-eyed."

It was pretty strong coffee.

"He must bear well the wintry weather."

No problem. This floatation suit keeps out the worst of the weather, although there is this annoying leak I meant to fix that lets the rain down the back of my neck…

Hm. Perhaps I'd not be so quick to judge next time.

After that first dab things quietened off considerably and the temperature eased itself further downward. True, there was to be no chance of a great journey from beneath my umbrella, but neither was I quite ready to go home yet. Perhaps there was still time to add another detail or two to the session.

There was no rush anyway as this place was mine now; it had been added to the collection, and whether this was through discovery or adoption it mattered little. Places like these are important – the often unvisited or forgotten corners tucked away like secret pockets in an old coat. Like these pockets that turn up old shopping lists and hand-scrawled notes that cryptically allude to an event long since lost to time and memory, there's just enough that is familiar about them to maintain interest, but just as much of the unknown that piques the curiosity.

I'd like to think that had Basho been there with me, huddled under the umbrella's nylon rather than in one of the bashō huts built for him by admirers, he'd have appreciated my little stand and its attempt to soldier on and finish the session. Perhaps he'd have leaned over and uttered a few wise observations to while away the hours whilst everywhere around us the snow kept falling, its cherry blossom flakes, endless beginnings, drifting like little asterisks through the night.

Wait, stars

Wait, stars, as I try to set this straight:
you not only illuminate
the night sky as we navigate
the darkened byways of our lives,
you also somehow orchestrate
our every fear, ambition, love,
to some distant celestial date
far beyond what our understanding may conceive.

Now, winds, whichever way you blow,
in whatever directions you may go,
this much, at least, can be held up as true –
you'll always find the quickest route,
never going around us but straight through,
so delicately taking us apart
that we never seem to realise how
you've laid open the quiet corners of our hearts.

Come, clouds, start your silent advance
and, with your subtle cadences
insinuate those half-imaginings
in shades of what we think we know we saw.
Smudge out a path across the skies
and down the half-lit slopes of dawn.
Come, laden with your inconsistencies.
Colour our waking with your undertones.

II – The Growing Year

Notes from the Margins

If directly asked what kind of angler I would primarily consider myself to be, I would invariably respond with the words 'sea angler'. But this is not entirely true, or at least not as accurate as it could be. I can be even more specific than this and refer to myself as a 'shore angler'.

Despite the lure of bigger fish, more variety, the possibility of more numerous shoals, and the swift undercurrents of deep water measured in fathoms rather than feet and inches, I can honestly say that boat angling has, so far, held no real appeal for me.

The sea disturbs me. I have no phobia of it, and never have I been afraid of coming into contact with it and yet, whenever I'm near the sea, looking out over its blankness, I suddenly feel very aware, and wary, of its capabilities. Every time I start to fish, particularly on rough nights, I spare a few seconds to think of all those lost – those anglers that have fallen from cliffs or were pulled in by rogue waves. I think of them, and shiver slightly at the thought of walking out of my house, kissing my wife and daughter goodbye and disappearing forever, another number lost to the waters. To be aboard a boat means that trust is not only placed in the skipper, the engine and the integrity of the hull, but also on the sea itself and, much as I may love the sea, I have never trusted it. There is no negativity in this though, as I find that this adds a certain amount of intrigue, particularly in those places I tend to spend most of my time - where the land meets the sea.

Were you to come back in from the featureless grey expanse of the open sea and instead follow the British coastline, I mean really follow every mile, in a plane, then the eye would be drawn along a virtually unending chain of torn edges: the rough, rock-ripped coastlines of Wales, the craggy expanses of the West country's Jurassic ledges, all those winding tatters of shingle stretching along the south coast around to Kent and so on. All frayed shreds indicating where an island that was once not an island had been ripped from its origins. Where there are straight lines there is plain fact and order, but where there is a ragged tag-end there is an unfinished story, the ongoing fragments of a narrative that bleeds in from the oceans and spins itself into the unravelled margins of our little island.

Webster's English dictionary defines the word 'margin' as:

'n. a border, edge'

And, although somewhat economic in its use of detail, this is beautifully adequate not only for the purpose of describing my angling mentality, but also for just about everything that surrounds it at this time of year.

It is midwinter. Imbolc or, more in keeping with our modern interpretation of faith, Candlemas, has only recently passed. Spring is both a distant memory and a tantalisingly longed-for near future. The worst of the freezing weather seems to be behind us, taking the first few steps of a grudging retreat. Temperatures have nudged ever so slightly upward and everywhere I look the world is starting to undergo its annual rehabilitation, going about the long business of remembering itself. The mini peach tree in the garden has led the way, the first to carry that extra tint of green, soon followed by the lavender and fuchsia. Everything lies limp and sodden like a cardboard food packet retrieved from the freezer, and one tentative foot is stepping toward spring, but as it is yet to make the first full leap of faith, we must be content for the moment to remain caught in a limbo somewhere between the frosts and the flowers.

Aside from the possibility of a spring run, the cod season is now almost over. The tight-knit group of anglers that forms the unofficial Brotherhood of the Cod disbands for the next six months and suddenly, many anglers find themselves cut free, dropped at the border of a strange country with the realisation that, for the time being at least, they have nowhere in particular to go and very little idea of how they are going to get there.

The big fish have all moved offshore to spawn; pickings are scant, limited to a few pin whiting and rockling. Almost unexpectedly, those overlooked tiddlers, the shoreline's bit-part players, shuffle tentatively to centre stage, and we are forced to become less selective in our search for a fish, any fish.

In such circumstances anglers, particularly those who are not catching anything, can very quickly become the most haunted of people.

They are haunted by their angling present. Are they fishing the right spot? Have they lost their touch? Are they using the correct rigs and baits and hooks?

They are haunted by their angling past; not the failures, but the successes. These baits have all caught in the past, and these marks have all produced fish, so what's different now?

Finally, they are haunted by their angling sessions yet to come. Future choices are doubted before they are even made; the paths that seemed so clear a month ago become confusing and directionless as the fog of uncertainty filters in.

I recall one such instance happening to me a few years back, as it nearly drove me to the outermost depths of despair. Through the best part of a month I couldn't so much as buy a bite while those around me seemed to catch an endless stream of obliging fish – flounders, codling, whiting; the capture of each of these fish was, of course, laced with the altruistic concern of the fellow angler:

"Watch you don't use up all your bait catching those fish, Si."

"Bucket's filling up nicely, mate."

I tried everything from snood length to hook size to casting range and all the rig and sinker combinations in between, reducing myself to an overwrought wreck in the process. After much swearing, hours of soul searching, threats, exhortations and, finally, prayers, I gave up. I'd had enough. And then, out of nowhere, it happened. Or maybe I just stopped trying so hard and allowed it to happen. Either way, as things annoyingly tend to do, it all just clicked into place, as though everything were just one part of one great big plan I'd only just stumbled across.

I reeled in my rig ready to pull off the mushed remnants of the lugworm I'd been fishing with when it gave a little jump in my hands. In disbelief I opened my fingers and there, in the beam of my headlight, a tiny flounder flipped around, desperate to be released. I nearly kissed it but was interrupted by ironic cheers from my left.

"What is it, Si?" came the shouts.

"Angel fish!" I replied. Shooting a quick glance skywards, I could almost have believed it too.

Like I did back then, some will fish on regardless, blindly plugging away; others will simply give up, pack their gear away for a few months and practise their golf swing while they wait for the summer season to begin. These days I usually choose to sit on the fence, getting out as and when the mood takes me.

This lull in the quality of the available fishing does carry one positive, however, in the fact that it affords me the luxury of spending a little more time walking the valley that stretches away a few streets behind my home, to follow the river upstream for ten minutes before being presented with another choice.

I could take the left-hand path, like most others, and follow the pavement that loops up onto the main road before bending back inward to curve around the rear of Ynys Park. I could circumvent the perimeter of the football pitch to the left and the river to the right, carried along on the shining black flow of the tarmac path, past the concrete fishing platform, continuing behind the new 'Copperminers' development, named as a testament to the livelihoods pursued in this valley over the years, and before I knew it I would be washed up into the village of Cwmavon.

Alternatively, I could opt for the right-hand path, and a much rougher, more shadowy route that winds its way through the shade of alder and larch. The ground here hardly ever dries, retaining a plasticine elasticity in all but the driest weather, and descending into a gloopy quagmire in the wet. But this is the one worth following, for this is the way of concealment.

Track through the tunnel of trees, breathing in the earthy aroma of wet leaf litter, adjusting your eyes to the sudden burst of shade, and you will find that this path allows closer contact with the river, obscuring the watcher behind small earth banks and branches, and bringing them almost to within touching distance of some of its inhabitants.

Amongst my favourites are the family of goosanders. For around the last five years they've been coming here to nest, raise chicks and fish this same length of river, using the same rocks as water breaks to gather themselves out of the main flow, the little chicks pootling through the slack water like black and white puffballs. Most walkers, keen to get from one end of the track to the other, or striding after a bounding dog, most often miss them entirely.

At certain times, like now, such unconsidered details become significant, especially for anglers. Anything considered a moot point in the more plentiful summer and autumn seasons transforms into potentially key information and I, like many others, am forced to refer to the historical, reaching back into my journals.

These journals are a fairly recent addition to my angling routine. When younger I rarely had the time or the inclination to bother with such details when there were fish to be caught, but over the last dozen years or so I have come to realise the value of noting the tides, winds, barometric pressure, bait and even moon phases that accompany every session.

When I sit down and take the time to look through some of the entries, I am immediately transported away to other times, other nights and other fish. Of course, the first and most obvious features to jump out from the pages are the photographs.

It's true that I am no Rembrandt with either brush or lens, but I am able to appreciate the value of a good image. Flicking through the pages of any issue of National Geographic, I can't help but marvel sometimes when confronted with a fiery bird's-eye view of a volcano, or a close-up of a tribesman on some dust plain, the care of all his life's years etched into his face like old rain channels in a parched riverbed. But can a picture ever truly be worth a thousand words? Surely, this is too uneven a bargain?

I have seen some truly superb angling photographs over the years, scenes that really capture the moment perfectly - a cod held above the frozen airborne droplets of the creaming chocolate surf from which it's just been pulled; the extreme close-up of a thornback ray's eye that that reflects elements of the world it stares out upon, and gives it back as a strange, alien landscape. But despite the obvious visual appeal, they are still no more than a brief instant held forever still like a stopped clock, a moth pinned behind glass, forever separated from their life and essence.

If it's this sense of life and essence that is needed, then it is to words that we must turn. All those verb tenses, the drive and direction of adverbs and the glorious adjectival facets impart to words a life that pictures simply cannot communicate.

Words don't always need that *tah-dah!* flashiness to get the message across. Take the brilliant Hemingway micro story:

For Sale. Baby shoes, never worn.

Sometimes words can swiftly become far more than they seem; those moments when, like a dying star, they begin to carry a weight and significance disproportionate to their size. When this happens, they can hurt and heal; they have the power to revive, to recall, to open understanding and, most of all, to define and flesh out life's minutiae and marginalia.

Just the other day, googling a plant I had noticed growing on a small patch of derelict ground turned up the name Goldenrod, a label I had heard before, yet it was still nice to put a name to the mental image I had of the plant. Now though, I was also armed with the knowledge that it also occasionally served as a tea, a good luck symbol and even a herbal remedy (should I ever need treatment for tuberculosis or a reduced flow of urine I shall know where to look).

But a little more reading immediately took me beyond the plant itself, the noun turning up Goldenrod as a colour. It's there in the charts, I promise you; wedged somewhere in the middle of *Mikado, Jonquil* and *Sunglow*, as though *Yellow* were simply not enough to adequately describe sunrises, cornfields and everything that shimmers in between. *Such a neat sideways sleight* I thought to myself. *No more than a slip of the brush bleeding across somebody's palette that became another thing in itself, a pretty way around the heart of the matter.* Apparently, it's representative of success, prosperity and happiness, so perhaps I should tuck some down into a corner of my tackle box next time I head out.

All of which brings me back to these rudimentary jottings in my journal. In each description, in every word, there lies a hidden lode of memories conveying every event and unexpected occurrence, no matter how small, just waiting to be tapped into.

One perfect example of this is an entry for March 2006. I had always fished my local beach over the high-water period, following the tide up from the low water line as, traditionally, that was when it had always fished well for me. On this particular day though, an opening after five weeks without fishing meant that my only opportunity would be for a short session over the last of the ebb tide and the first of the flood.

The weather was windless and flat calm and, to top it all, this session would be fished in the doldrums of March, that sea angling dead zone where even the dabs have departed. It had *disaster* and *blank* written all over it, but three hours and a couple of dozen rockling, pin whiting and pouting later, I had enough material to fuel my late winter/early spring sessions for years to come. Due mainly to this lesson, I have learned to scribble down every minor little thing, no matter how scrappy or scant, as it is from such jottings that genuine discoveries are often made. As Arthur Conan Doyle put it: "Life is infinitely stranger than anything which the mind of man could invent".

Looking back through the various sections over the years, I have begun to see how true this is, stumbling across many such forgotten gems like

'Beach fished well on a NW wind compared to a blank last time on SW wind. 1 codling, a sole a bass and 3 small-eyed rays'

And the particularly fortuitous

'Nothing until a miscast, sandeel bait dropped at 15 yards. Hit by 3lb 4oz bass'.

Subsequent entries showed that I was able to capitalise on this, catching eight bass over two pounds in two sessions by using the same tactics.

Flicking through these notes is like carrying out a conversation with myself, theses old sentences recalling to mind every fish and each decision that went into catching it. But the notes do not come from me. Each time I cast out a line, this is where the real conversation is opened, one in which I have no idea what will happen or what, if anything, will tune in through the surf's white noise.

Just upriver from the estuary for instance, the mullet are usually ponderous in their response, considering for what seems an age any point offered to them, in total contrast to the smash-and-grab full stop of the bass or the usual affirmative double nod-nod of the codling. Some discussions are too long to be conducted quickly and need frequent refocusing, such as the elliptical rap-rap-rap a shoal of whiting offers when they are not so rudely interrupted by the curmudgeonly, insistent interferences of the occasional dogfish.

And sometimes, as now, there will be no response at all, and the rod tips will remain motionless. Perhaps I've been a little too vague, or maybe it's time to go back to my notes, just to check one or two of those minor details. Never mind, I think it's just one of those days – a little bit mint, a touch clary sage.

Just

Just then –
a subtle sound,
a turn of air.

Or a turn in my thoughts.
I catch things readjusted,
just so, although
I could have sworn to an arrival,

Quick, you know,
something like a hawk
threading a forest's tangled boles
(only just),

And that swerve,
that bright verve
left its trace
here
and
here
in the stream's clear lacing,
the pagan thrust of green;
green is the grass;
green are the leaves;
green is the seam
that starts in this,
just this
just now.

Just.

Weather-eye

I - Storm

A couple of days ago, a bank of grey cloud came rolling high over the hills behind the town, a foggy surf table that rose and then descended to break over the streets. One moment people, houses, cars and buildings scuttled around at its leading edge like so much flotsam, the next the town lay silent in a misted shroud of hush as a mizzle settled in, ready to last for the following couple of days.

In this most changeable of seasons, there's none of the gradual ornate dismantling of the visual landscape as there is in autumn, no leaf-by-leaf taking down of the old to make way for the new. The murky blankness comes and everything else goes in this seasonal game of all-or-nothing.

The mist drifted into the space between our front window and the street outside like an ash haze. Later, while walking over to the shops, the streetlights and car headlights seemed momentarily a little brighter, as though kicking out in reaction to this smothering, but their pale, impotent glow was soon swallowed back up in the watery grey until those lights seemed to lose each other and drift further apart again, a distant galaxy dispersed in perspective.

A national obsession, the weather has become so deeply entrenched in our culture and our literature that it has become something of a personality all of its own, with its differing moods and personas and quirks. In some cases, it is depicted as the sullied villain of the piece as in Ted Hughes' poem *Wind*, the wind itself a guilty rogue with a wild and unpredictable nature, whereas in others we see the eerie strangeness of the silent invader, supernaturally drifting through James Joyce's story *The Dead*, his character Gabriel Conroy hearing seeming to hear in '…the snow falling faintly through the universe', something reaching beyond mere weather into the metaphysical ether. Either way, there generally lurks a peculiar and unpredictable otherness about the weather and the way it 'falls' or 'closes in' or 'comes down' like the unexpected interloper, its schizophrenic temperament fluctuating all the time.

Being quite fond of this unusual, interchangeable time of year, I am fully aware that it's an enthusiasm I may not share with many others. My wife Rachel, for instance, is a sun lover, and always has been. Where she loves lying in the sun I prefer to hide in cooler rooms through the summer. Spool the year on a few months to the slow, fruitful hours that pile up at summer's back end though, and I come into my element while she enters a state of semi-hibernation, swaddled in bed socks and thick woollen cardigans. So, where I find a state of indecisive appeal at this time of year, I am acutely conscious of the fact that it can induce in others a state of irritability, shorter hours leading to blackened moods, cooler temperaments and dampened affability. This was the case last night, the wet, foggy conditions leading to confinement which, in turn, led to an occlusion of our moods, something that surged through the living room until, after nearly an hour of to-ing and fro-ing, we were deposited like castaways upon our own little islands of indignation at two very distant points, slightly disoriented and more than a little exhausted.

The room was full of the cloying atmosphere of annoyance so, the only solution to this being a blast of fresh air to clear the fug, I packed the car and went in search of some quiet space, heading out regardless of whatever the weather was doing.

A still-pregnant sky was awaiting my arrival at the beach, the first spots of rain arriving shortly afterward, recognised as a drumming against my hood. A lifeguard's flag strained and slapped against its pole as the wind fretted it, its guitar string squeal adding to the dismal seasonal mixtape that played in my head.

The rain's spattering began to intensify, each individual beat joining up until they finally formed one drubbing note just as I cast the first bait into the water and stood back to watch the rod tip in the midst of the mess of weather. In the downpour everything slowly began to soften out at the edges, including me, like a tiny background figure in a painting by an old master, blurring out beneath the shellac.

I endured this solid wall of rain, retreating back into my

clothing and reducing my world to one small viewing screen beneath my hood. Eventually, after forty-five minutes, the rain slowed, then stilled, and a brief period of quiet calm fell upon the beach, allowing me to take down the hood and open up my view of the world. As often happens in such quiet moments, fishing soon gave way to watching – the swirls and eddies of the tide up the face of the rocks to my left; a giant iron ore ship waiting out in the bay for the tug that would guide its bulk into the harbour to ready itself.

Then came the first faint flashes of lightning from the west.

At first there was the occasional flicker, and I watched as the sky over the West country began to fill again and the thunderclouds tumbled through the sky with the consistency of paint swirled from a brush into a jar of water.

I looked on as the storm moved rapidly, spreading first over Devon then expanding outward across Cornwall. Onward and outward it rolled, reaching further and further until I began noticing flashes beyond Swansea where the storm had begun to circle around me and approach from the west, over the Gower peninsula.

After having caught only a solitary dogfish, and reluctant to be caught in the vicinity of two fifteen-foot carbon poles when the lightning arrived, I wound in both rods and packed away for the night.

Where my arrival had seen the last of the daylight punctuated by the passing darkness of sudden squalls, now, from the car, I watched the night deepen and some of its individual features picked out by brief periods of illumination as the storm flared up angrily over the bay. I had been reading Frankenstein with a GCSE class earlier, and now felt a little like Victor Frankenstein, watching 'the tempest, so beautiful yet terrific', the 'noble war in the sky' until a dark shadow returned to taint my night again. Sometimes even angling isn't enough.

After another five minutes I started the car's engine. Time to go back home. The lightning flashed on, picking out, momentarily here and there, the little tug preparing to meet the incoming ship, and I was reminded of the little Breton Fisherman's Prayer that I keep taped to the inside of my tackle box:

Lord,
The sea is so wide
And my boat is so small.
Be with me.

I pulled off as the tug finally moved out of the harbour's safety, caught the tide, and began its efforts to span the divide.

II – Afterward

And so, peace is restored following last night's events. Perhaps not restored, but put back in place, a place that is outwardly very similar but in an alignment that can never be exactly the same again, adding another little nuance to our ever-changing subtext. Whereas we kept our distance last night, we now walk hand-in-hand along the shore, losing ourselves amongst the dog walkers and joggers. Although the worst of the storm passed with the night, there is still a stiff breeze now, all of the other walkers tucking their chins down into collars and scarves in an effort to avoid its bite.

Occasionally they glance up hopefully, but see not much of interest aside from a frothy, grey-brown churning scum in place of the calm sea next to which they'd hoped to walk. Even the expected airy, in-flight lines of a black-backed gull appear twisted and bunched as it hunches over a washed-up pin whiting, ripping its way into the body through the gills. Bleached-out sanitary products lay limply where the tide slapped them onto the sand.

It repulses these people, this other face that's always there but often hidden and hardly ever acknowledged; the schizophrenic flip-side that can cough up a horde of jellyfish or even, sometimes, a human being, with no more sentiment or thought than if they were carrier bags.

We walk on, content with the idea that this is how our little world has chosen to rearrange itself for now, foregoing the need to talk and instead listening - to what is familiar amongst the new - the surf, to the birds and the wind; listening and knowing that, although the days will always come again with new faces, they will always break and communicate what needs to be said with old, old voices.

Keeping Faith

'Sea sounds were the concomitant of Celtic prayer. Without sea-cadence, prayer to them sounded thin.'

- ***Ronald Blythe, River Diary***

I arrive from the western end: slowly, softly, a footpad stalking through the long tufts of marram. Their wet stems, loaded with the day's early dew, creak like eaves beneath my feet.

We are into the early flushes of spring, but still getting by on meagre rations for now, the watery gruel of sunlight in this early season still not enough to fully energise me after a long, drab winter. Tired, I still seem to travel as much by feel as by sight, a throwback to the late dawn/early dusk format of the winter days from which we are only just beginning to drag ourselves. I crest the first mound, half falling, half resisting in those giant bounding strides which, as kids, we usually reserve for those special times when playing in deep sand or a sudden dump of snow. Each new soft step I take rapidly infills behind me, an egg-timer trickling reminding me that I need to get this job done quickly before I get ready for work, but not so quickly that I don't have time to take a moment.

Putting the bucket down, I scan the scene, drinking in shadow and wind, movement and depth, involuntarily ending up back in a descriptive writing lesson I taught a group of year 10s yesterday. "When writing a piece of description" I tell my students, "there's one thing that you need to think about at all times. Just one thing that will make your writing really tick."

"Are you talking about similes sir? And metaphors?"

"That's good, Jonathan; they do help to a certain extent, but that's not what I'm talking about."

"The senses sir?" asks Chloe. "Using all five senses so that the reader can see and smell and hear everything in the scene?"

"That's a nice point too, Chloe. Really important. But it's not what I'm after. Anyone?" Rows of blank faces.

I go on to explain to them that life is the key ingredient – life in all its living, breathing, bright, dark, quiet, loud forms. "Without it" I say, "all you will ever produce is a very pretty, but very flat, painting made out of words. Lovely, but nothing more than a still image when there should be a blurring cascade of film." I try to go into more depth, explaining how we exist not just in space but in time, time that passes us in an ever-moving torrent of change: the tick of a clock; the movement of the sun across a wall; the rising of a tide. Although they produce some very nice pieces of writing, most of them lack the spark I'm speaking of. Marking the pieces later, I realised, not without a sense of irony, that this wasn't something that could be easily taught in a classroom. It was no lecture theatre theory that taught me what I try to teach others; it was actually being in places like this, at times just like this.

The eastern flanks of the sand dunes rising behind me catch the first of the early light like sunstruck gables, the penumbra at their wide concave bases slowly dissipating in a yellowy-white half-light that gradually dilutes into the morning's slow-growing dawning.

My journey presses on upstream. As the estuary funnels and narrows into the river, my progress meanders along with it so that I am pushed further upstream, past chunks of driftwood and and the dogged spikes of sea holly.

It is low tide now; I can smell it. There is nothing that can replicate the tang of the estuary at low tide, that unique mixture of muddy clay, ozone and rotting bladder wrack that worms its way into the head via the nostrils and refuses to let go. It is one of those few places, like a cool, damp wooded grove or agricultural fields mantled in their ammoniac reek of chicken shit, that are first experienced through smells and which, after that first encounter, are immediately locked away in the memory bank only to be dusted off years later when a chance visit to a similar place immediately sets the senses off on a journey across your Proustian mind map.

Finally, I reach the spot I'm looking for, its dark, glossy backdrop of river mud and its ossuary silence inhabiting the place as always. A strange image, perhaps, but then, no; an accurate one. Ever since I was a child this place has held the same kind of fascination that inhabited my imagination when roaming old churchyards: the skeletal frames of shopping trolleys quietly going about the collection of barnacles on their exposed ribs; sections of old net and fishing line jostled about by successive tides sounding a sinewy *twang* where they are stretched to breaking point by the tide's power, strung out between rocks and rotting wooden posts; large shining lumps of black slag littering the banks like chits of bone working their route to the surface of a Neolithic burial site.

Working quickly, I unclip the lid from my bucket and am immediately smacked about the head by the pungent stench of fish – sprats and mackerel – minced up with white bread and a dash of water to form an oily paste. Scrabbling around in the driftwood and loose pebbles littering the ground around my feet, quickly yields ten rounded, palm-sized pebbles to add weight. Around them, the oily fish paste is moulded until each ball is around the size of a fist, before each of them is hurled with a splash into the brown flow of the river's waters.

All of this – the time, the effort, the preparation, may all have been in vain. It's still perhaps a little early in the year for what I'm intending, although I have been successful around this time in past years. They might not come. Still, the offerings have been made, and now all I can do is wait, hope that the timing is right, and keep faith that they will make their appearance.

*

The day, like so many others, is blurred by work, nearly ten hours passing before I find myself in the same spot, marked out by the crumbling wooden stump, a rotting tooth protruding from the bank. Among a few such stumps this one is easily identified by the large rust-orange nail poking out, the spot where, nearly twenty years ago, I came across three eels skewered by the head and left to dangle as convicts on a gibbet. More than half my lifetime later and the image is still vivid in my mind, a reminder that, despite all our supposed cleverness and development, human beings are no more than animals after all.

The water is once again approaching low slack, so I take the opportunity to send out a few more of the fishy bread balls that sink straight to the bottom, accompanied by a few floating crusts to add some surface attraction. Not long now.

Looking around, I see that I am alone. In fact, it doesn't appear that many people, if any, have been here all day. This is a place where noise is not required. Here, silence loses its sideline status as a mere space filler and becomes dominant, something to be kept and valued as an integral presence.

Five minutes pass.

Ten.

Fifteen.

Small fragments of detritus begin to float back inward from the sea; the fresh influx of water fleshes out the few remaining channels until they begin to pulse like capillaries. The handful of trawlers and small charter boats are nudged awake from their half-drunk listing.

Not yet. No, not yet.

Keep your eyes open; wait.

Soon. If they are going to come, it will be soon.

The water gently laps up against the rock bank I'm standing on. Twenty feet out, there's…no; just a scrap of wood.

Shit! A sudden clacking cacophony makes my heart leap suddenly as a pair of gulls squirl and squabble over a few scraps of mackerel skin and briefly snatch my attention.

Shadows. Everywhere I look I seem to see shadows and shapes that shift and twist just beneath the surface:

a tatty old carrier bag here,
      a length of pipe lagging there;
            ripples
                more ripples
                    a tiny eddy
                        a puff of mud

and then, from the corner of my eye, I see them.

They come.
    Just one at first,
        then another,
            and then they shiver into view like grey ghosts.

These wise old men of the estuary have no need to rush; they come pondering through the silty waters, over the mudflats and the crab holes, the worm beds and the man-made clutter. Rising to the surface they mouth their silent credos over and over again, utterances that echo noiselessly to join the endless flow. I allow myself a brief smile.

There are few fish swimming in British saltwater that can command the devotion received by the mullet. A true sporting fish, it wields a quiet power and knowingness in the British sea angler's imagination that ensures the return of the acolytes year after frustrating year.

I move away from the water's edge, avoiding any chance of skylining myself and spooking them. So absorbed have I been in my vigil that I've forgotten to tackle up. One clumsy mistake now could unravel all the hours of preparation. In situations like this even my own shadow might become an enemy.

The mullet is a quiet fish, a seemingly contemplative fish, a wary fish, so tackle is used sparingly – a size eight hook, a small clear bubble float and a sandy-coloured specialist carp line chosen for its thinness to strength ratio and the fact that the colour will vanish into the murk of the estuary. A small section of soft white bread is pinched around the hook and cast thirty yards uptide, allowing the bait to trundle slowly back toward me on the tide.

Only a handful of minutes have slipped into the slow turning of the afternoon's wheels when something catches me off guard by suddenly rising and engulfing the bait with a big wet *WALLOP!* Instinctively the rod sweeps up with a rapier swish and ...keeps going, describing an almost perfect half circle as I theatrically miss the bite and nearly end up on my back.

*

Nearly ninety fishless minutes later and I'm still reliving every movement of that bite, especially the fact that, in missing it, I spooked the fish and cleared the swim. There would have been no sense in fishing on immediately, so it was a case of watching and waiting for the fish to begin showing again.

The water became considerably deeper and faster-moving, so fishing on with the float would have been useless anyway. I decide it's time to tackle down and go home. Or is it? Glancing across the river, I slurp on the last dregs of my tea whilst watching a boat owner who rowed across from the bank with the rising tide to tinker about between the tiny wheelhouse and the deck; organising, sweeping, flicking scraps overboard in some rusty, mud-caked industrial Welsh rendering of a Constable scene.

The boats! Why didn't I think of it earlier?

There is, perhaps, one more chance.

Further upstream, where the estuary narrows into the river, the fish will be funnelled past the main mooring area where they might congregate for a while around the submerged hulls before heading even further upstream. The decision is made in a second and five minutes later I'm plopping a legered rig out right next to the nearest of the small boats.

There's no time for daydreaming, thankfully, as the next bite comes quickly, swinging the rod tip around hard and fast. This is the great paradox of the mullet - it saunters up and down the estuary with all the ponderous acumen of a bourgeois intellectual but attach it to the end of a fishing line and it will go fin to toe like a half-cut docker, never giving so much as an inch without scrapping over it first.

The fish immediately runs off across the tide and then turns uptide, dragging line with it. There are no obvious snags in that direction so I give the fish its head and let it run, hoping it will start to tire itself. Realising that it's going nowhere, it turns and hares back toward the boats and their mooring ropes and I reverse the rod just in time to exert enough side strain as the mullet hammers its head, *jag-jag-jag*, in the direction it wants to go, causing the rod's fine quiver tip to nod appreciatively at its power; back and forth, on and on, the fish ploughs deeply through the brown tide in front of me until, after what seems an arm-aching eternity, there is a silvery roll just beneath the surface. It's almost time.

One more turn and it's on the surface; at around three and a half pounds it's not a big fish by any means, but muscular and serious, decked out in its sober, scholarly hues. For all the tussling, considering the violence of the take and the early fight, the mullet finally capitulates gently enough as I drop to one knee and slide it softly over the lip of the next.

The sun continues its descent toward the horizon, tinting this natural sandy basin with a shimmering backcloth of orange, brown and silver, reducing me to little more than a silhouette that, from the heights of the dunes behind, must look for all the world like that of a man stooping to prayer.

Lost and Found

The back door opens just a crack, then a touch more as I try to gauge the weather. It's nearing summer, true, but an early chill creeps across the skin, raising little millipede-print goose bumps as it goes. I hunch in a little closer around the coffee mug.

A movement. Somewhere out in the garden's pooled murk a shadow twists and pulls itself free from the darkness around it and the cat slinks up to rub against my leg as she oozes through the door into the kitchen. Sometimes she'll leave a little gift – a mouse; a vole – but no gift tonight. I down the last of my coffee, click off the light and give everything back to the black.

Everyone is asleep; everyone inside and, it seems, outside. It is time to leave. The front door slides closed with a *shhh*, the car's engine grumps awake and I'm away.

It's early, and yes, ideally, I'd like to be tucked up in bed right now, but this is the deal, this is how everything simply fits. I am the composite man: husband, father, teacher, angler; all roles I must fulfil and must balance in whatever way I can. For now, the role of teacher is put to one side as the half-term holiday is here, but this only places greater emphasis on everything else. There will be meals to eat, bottles of wine to share and walks to take as a husband; there will be trips to swimming pools and cinemas and parks as father, and so, before he is lost somewhere in the middle of it all, I fit the angler in wherever I can, even if that leads me along an empty stretch of motorway at three in the morning.

Other cars are few and far between. All this empty road creates a sense of a world in which the last great age of mankind has played out to a shuddering halt. Miles tick by unhindered and were it not for the voices coming through the radio, all would be silent. The scenery does little to elevate the mood, the blurred backdrop robbing the wayside of any romance, inverting Dick Walker's famously beautiful vigil scene to leave me in a vista of grey and black and blue. Amidst such murk and regularity, it's easier to notice the chaotic straggles of colour, even by sodium light, that are haphazardly sellotaped to the railings at various points along the motorway and the A-roads. These floral tributes are an unnatural bloom, left to wither as reminders of once-flourishing lives snuffed out too soon.

The lack of traffic sees me arrive at the shore in good time. The beachside apartment blocks all around the car park are dark, save for the insomniac glare of a few lighted windows.

Dozens and dozens of flats surround me like the cells of an abandoned hive. When alive during the day, this place can often seem insanely busy, but at night it becomes the opposite, its walls and windows offering nothing back but a muffled, dead echo as I take the spade and bucket from the boot, pull on my willies, flick on the headlamp and trudge out to the worm bed.

I'm not alone. Someone's already here - a professional. I can tell he's a professional bait digger by the short, blocked shadows scattered around him – buckets. Even the way he digs marks him out. All around him are the darker recesses of the curved trenches he has dug to drain away excess water as he methodically works his way through the worm bed, far more organised than my dipping in and out method of digging one worm at a time. He hasn't noticed me as he's too engrossed in his work, but I watch awhile, wondering about him.

Slowly, rhythmically, he moves as though locked into some bizarre repetitive dance routine - dipping, rising, turning, shuffling on; dipping, rising, turning, shuffling on. I envy him, thinking how satisfied he must be in such a life, spared the usual constraints of the nine-till-five grind, out on the shoreline in an environment he loves, getting some exercise whilst being paid to take part in an activity that has always been his lifeblood.

Quickly though, I give myself a talking-to when I realise that I'm romanticising the scene to some ridiculous level, projecting my own ideals and feelings onto someone about whom I know absolutely nothing. He's probably knackered by having to work around these early tides for a pittance and would probably kill for some comfy desk job paying a decent wage; a job with a pension at the end of it and no half-broken back to limit his spending it. Any love he might have had for all of this was most likely sweated out years ago.

I watch him for a while, thinking about what might have led him here. Choice? Disaffection in his school days? A little beer money on the side? Again though, any attempt to understand would be all me, so I give it up. It's not my place to know or understand action and rhythm and routine, well-practised and worked deep down into the muscles and the memory.

The set of constraints by which he lives are common to the world around him – the tides, the weather, all those things that affect his day-to-day survival are those that affect everything else that lives from the shoreline, from the birds, to the fish, to the shellfish deep in the sand upon which he walks and, although I have come to know places like this well through the years, I shall never know them, or be tied to them, half so closely as him.

With a last searching rake of his hands he plucks a final couple of worms from the beach, throws a few broken-off tails to the gulls lurking nearby then straightens up, pressing his hands into the small of his back. As he stacks and picks up his buckets, he spots me. Without missing a beat, he throws a perfunctory nod in my direction before picking up his buckets and striding off.

I suddenly realise I haven't dug a single thing yet.

Lugman

Out on the strand
the tide is turning,
but he's not done.

Not quite.

There's always time for a few more
in the bucket,
the day's reckoning;
true success squirms in the hand,
is measured by the pound.

Out on the strand
he turns to it again,
opening the sand,
spine straining in time with
the handle's creaking rhythm,
always just this side of broken.

His life's work's sunk deep
into these empty foundations.

Their blunt wind-walls
encircle him.

III – Year's Fullness

Cry Havoc!

There's no sign yet. The sea is almost completely unruffled aside from an ever-changing chop where the sun has already begun working out its endless geometries – a triangular fleck of yellow here, a rhombus of white there, then gone in an instant.

The mid-range tide lacks any swell, or at least anything recognisable as swell aside, perhaps, from a just perceptible flensing of the surface until it butts up against the natural rampart of the rock promontory under my feet. I have timed my arrival to catch the ebb tide. Its lowering, like the subtle changing of so many things in life, is barely noticeable, indicated only by the marks left behind where a dark band an inch above the water tracks along the entire length of the rocks.

Still, there's time enough to take a minute before setting up, what with today being the longest day. Yesterday's news was full of last year's recycled pictures of druids and new age travellers dancing and praying in front of Stonehenge, backlit by a corona. They'll have been celebrating in Wiltshire for a few hours, but I thought I'd fritter away a few of these daylight hours and take my time this morning.

Others have chosen the same mark as me today, meaning that there are a number of us lined up hoping for an abundance – of sunshine, of scenery and, hopefully, of fish. Peaceful as this summer morning might be, I know that it isn't entirely placid as the solstice is not the only event around here at the moment. For a week the smoke signals and jungle drums have increased in intensity, reporting running skirmishes. Snatched whispers here and odd snippets of information there all report guerrilla style smash and grab raids followed by swift disappearances all along the coast, but as the facts are carefully pieced together, a picture is emerging.

They are coming.

The tackle has been carefully selected for today, all sturdy items up to the task: durable beachcasters and high-speed reels for battling hard-fighting fish over their chosen terrain.

The tide has really started to push back now and it's time to begin. Simply pulling the bucket toward me stimulates a chorus of tiny scratching noises – crabs. To many, when the smooth hounds arrive, the only bait worth even looking at is crab. Hermit crabs, peeler crabs, hardbacks; it doesn't really matter as these fish are indiscriminate in their tastes. For millions of crabs every year, possibly the last thing they see is the brief passing of a shadow before they are suddenly smashed and devoured by the packs.

Over the years I have also caught them on ragworm and squid so I'm compromising to see what they're looking for today. For the first rod I quickly cut a common hardback shore crab in half and whip both halves around the hook with elastic, ensuring an instant blast of crabby smell wafting down the tide. For the second rod I'm going for a slower more gradual approach. The empty body cavity of a squid is stuffed with smashed crab, whipped closed at the top with elastic and mounted on a pennell rig. This is punctured three or four times to allow the scents to slowly mingle and gradually seep away. Both rigs are lobbed to around seventy yards - no need for exaggerated casting styles or fancy technique here. The drags are loosened, the ratchets set and it's simply a case of keeping watch.

Expectations always run a little high during these sessions, so it's never a surprise when the reality doesn't live up to the hope. Still, that still doesn't ease the disappointment of the first two hours being fishless. The sun is blazing down through the windless air and it doesn't take long before a soporific haze sets in and my mind absently begins to wander so that the tiniest detail can hold the attention, even though it may not be particularly interesting – a small flotilla of gulls bobbing gently on the oily water are reduced to negative background shades by an empty KP Skips packet split open, its gaudy colours reminiscent of a drowned bird of paradise.

Just a couple of hundred yards further along another angler has been set up for the last hour, and scanning across now, I can see that he's into a fish - his beachcaster has been hooped over into its fighting curve. I watch the tussle unfold as he's clearly forced to give line a few times; it's a good fish and it fights him all the way.

I'm so busy watching this as though in a dream that I'm catapulted into consciousness by the sudden cry of alarm that rises from the vicinity of my own rods when a ratchet screams in alarm, its coarse vibrato tearing through the air as a fish rips line from the reel.

The smooth hound is a fish that demands respect and demands it immediately. Unlike the simply unfolding narrative of, say, the flounder bite or a float caught Pollack, hooking a smooth hound can be compared to watching an entire two-hour film in five minutes. Even the calmest temperament can fold like a cheap umbrella. Things that have been checked and double-checked before now seem ridiculously ill-prepared: I suddenly seem to be miles from my rods; gear that I thought was laid out neatly and to hand now seems to be strewn everywhere, and I almost fall over the bait bucket as I sprint, or attempt to sprint, over the uneven ground between me and the rods.

Amazingly, I make it to the rods in one piece, click the reel into gear and am instantly connected to what feels like a horse galloping in the opposite direction. The rod is nearly wrenched from my hand as I fumble with the ratchet, trying to adjust the drag as I do so. Even when I find it, it makes little difference as line continues to pour from the spool, only now the scene is muted. There is a brief lull after the initial twenty-yard run as the fish, obviously the intended target, cuts across the tide, and I am able to pump and wind under strain, carefully cranking five or six yards of line back onto the spool before the fish decides that enough is enough and takes off again. Of the seven other anglers I can see, four are also into fish; we are like greedy schoolboys trying to take our fill and more, and why not? If others haven't come to take advantage of this glut, then it's their loss!

Everything, every nerve, every sinew, every knot and even the hook itself comes under immense strain from this muscular wrestler of a fish. The power of a smooth hound is not easily described and has to be felt to be truly believed. Above all, it must be respected – any weaknesses are soon found out. The drag has been carefully set and the fish can take line, though I am never out of control, but this doesn't account for the unseen dangers. Despite the higher vantage point of the rocky perch on which I'm standing, and my powerful fifteen-foot beachcaster working like a shock absorbing lever as I swing it left or right to direct the fish, there's a teeth-jangling sensation of grating as the fish drags the line over an unseen snag.

Unexpectedly, everything goes solid for a second. Tentatively, I give the line a little tug first one way then the other in the vain hope that I can gently free the rig, when there is an abrupt surge and the rig pulls itself free, zipping back and forth in front of me again, though the runs now lack any real power.

The smoothhound is working hard now, forced to fight the rod, the reel's drag, and the angler holding them, and another few shorter lunges all but spend the last reserves of the fish's energy. By this time, I'm sweating hard and half-shaking with the adrenalin, but the fight is swinging in my favour.

For the first time it breaks the surface in front of me and I'm able to get a good look at it and I am struck by the similarity to Ted Hughes' description of a pike, how every single part of it seems perfected and honed, because looking at a smooth hound is to look at nature's own variation on the torpedo. I picture this fish as an *everyfish*, swimming the oceans through the millennia, the water eroding and smoothing away all superfluous edges and protuberances until it left only this. Millions of years of evolutionary trial and error focused down to the fine needlepoint in place and time that is this creature swimming in front of me at this moment, this perfection of a simple design shown off to best effect in the sleek flanks and angular lines containing a compromise between speed and raw power. Particle by particle the apex predator is sculpted rather than born.

I'm fairly high up, and the fish is still moving, so it's hard to estimate an exact size, but it looks to be somewhere in the region of the nine-pound mark, maybe pushing double figures. By now I'm feverishly looking for a way down to the water's edge, keeping a holding pressure on the fish, when out of nowhere there's a sudden sickening lurch and I tumble backwards, arms wheeling, left connected to nothing but air, before tumbling onto my backside on a rough outcrop of rock. I get to my feet just in time to see the fish swirl back out to sea.

This is the gut-wrenching reality that is the lost fish. As I wind in the empty rig, I mentally run through all the possibilities in my head – had the taut line come into contact with a rock? Was one of my knots below standard? The reality was revealed when the rig hit the rocks beneath my feet and I noticed that the strong 3/0 blacked Aberdeen hook, not a cheap or weak hook by any means, was twisted out of shape, had lost its black finish in places and now resembled nothing more than the half-digested leg bones of a shrew or vole sticking out from a casually discarded owl pellet.

I don't know whether to laugh or cry. There is some small comfort in the fact that I actually got to see the fish, but that nagging of so near yet so far…

Still, I've enough spare rigs, lots of crabs and there are hours of daylight left. I've got a feeling that this is going to be a long day.

Foreigners

Dawn has yet to break fully over the silhouetted hills behind me. It will make little difference when it does anyway. I am tucked out of sight between the rocks, hovering only three feet from the surface of the water, water so calm that, if I concentrate for a moment, I can make out finer details in my wavering reflection: bags under the eyes and a slight rash of stubble, the signs of missed sleep and an early start. The cloying damp and the tang of ozone thicken around me like last night's soup in this dank nook.

Despite the month, it is cold. There will be little to differentiate July from November until the sun has been up for a few hours, but I am prepared for the wait. Travelling light, I am almost nomadic in my body warmer; I carry only a bucket and a light rod, my grandfather's tattered canvas knapsack, containing a small flask of tea and a few odds and ends, slung over my shoulder.

Nothing moves in the windless morning; not even the wind stirs. Every small sound I make ricochets from rock to rock and echoes out from this craggy enclave. This close to the water, every move I make must be quiet, stealthy, the sinuous connivings of a stoat on a riverbank. Slowly I slip the plastic box from my bag, sliding out a pre-cut chunk of mackerel. It's easier this way - less movement and fuss when the bait is prepared at home in those excited, sleepless hours before this kind of session.

The hook is threaded in and out of the bait a few times, leaving the point proud in anticipation of the moment when a bass may slam into the simple rig, allowing the needle-sharp barb to drive home. Good. A gentle, pendulum-like swing and the baited hook slips into the water with a faint plop only five or six yards from where I am perched. The ripples recede, everything settles once again into silence and my friend and I, thirty yards apart, are simply absorbed back into the gloom.

Out along the length of the distant promenade, the first simple stirrings of life flit around the solitary outlines of early strollers and dog walkers stumbling through the dawn's initial blush. We wait on.

*

By ten o' clock the world has fully woken, both the tide and the sun have risen considerably and we're no longer alone. In the passage of only a few hours the first of the others have started to materialise and come to settle around us; at various points, blunt white torsos chipped into shape by long periods of exposure to the sun have begun to appear on the tips of the outermost rocks where they stand and face silently out to sea.

Another twenty minutes slip by and nothing but a handful of mackerel and eels interrupt the gentle cadence of the morning; they are swung in juddering and quickly, but gently, released back into the water. We have not come for them today.

More have come to populate the platforms around me, the nearest bodies marked with inked-out patchworks of multi-coloured whorls and serpentine coils, tribal insignias flickering across flesh pierced and glinting. Behind this, the steady throb of R and B blurs the air as a long, snaking line, gaudy in summer colours and loaded down with boxes, buckets and bags, undulates along the breakwater toward us, quivering slightly in the building heat.

Other noises have now begun to rise above the music. A group of Polish lads twenty feet away buzz in a swarm of their vowels and soft consonants; an Indian man barks at his two young boys as they skitter about and chatter like macaques, all wide smiles and impish action. A Chinese family further up towards the end huddle into themselves, relaxed and flicking low susurrant whispers to each other.

The languages and dialects merge into a dense mesh around us as the mackerel, the bounty for which they have all turned up, start to come in thick and fast. The whole pier is a vibrant thrum of industrious activity, arms thrown forward and back as lines are cast toward the sea, the steady sink and draw of the rods calling to mind the steam-driven pistons of a Victorian dockyard or factory as dozens of mackerel, scad and lithe, flexing garfish are hauled efficiently from the water in dangling, pearlescent strings, to disappear kicking away their last percussive moments in rustling bin liners and Tesco carrier bags.

Finally, it happens. The rod jerks alive in my hands and is almost wrenched from my fingers as it makes a sudden jagging lunge down towards the sea. The line sings that eerie single note that always thrills down the back of my neck like icy fingers, raising the fine hairs as I lean back into the fish, watching the line zig zag in and out from the rocks in a living cardiograph, then swoop around in ever smaller circles. All this waiting and it's over almost as quickly as it began. Two minutes of struggle, a few yards of line, some head shakes and crash-dives and I "have colour" in front of me: first a quick, bright flash and then a solidifying flex into shape and depth just beneath the water as the bass emerges just beneath the surface like a car following its own headlights through fog. Soon after, I'm guiding the bass over the lip of the waiting net in front of me.

We skip from the rocks to the flat concrete surface above to weigh our prize, what turns out to be a four-pound bar of silver flaring in the midday light, all shimmering scales and armour-plated spikes.

Looking up we notice for the first time how drastically the breakwater has been transformed. Deckchairs, tents, umbrellas and cool boxes are scattered in a multi-coloured shambles under plumes of cigarette smoke. Everywhere, beers are being opened, glistening bodies are reclining in chairs and along the concrete, splayed out in the heat; shouts layer over shouts as the smells of sun cream and hot flesh permeate the air and mingle in their warm biscuit aroma whilst the breakwater shimmers like a souk in the sun.

Now all eyes are suddenly on us, two strangers dressed in jeans, body warmers and boots who have appeared from nowhere. Out in the open, away from our shady little enclave, I realise how hot it has become and how much we're sweating now in our seemingly ill-suited clothing. I remember that I am still holding something this day has not yet seen, the only thing we came for. Everybody crowds around for a closer look. Closer still. The crowd parts then seals itself behind me as I pass, continuing to watch. The comments begin to come: "She's a corker", "He's a lovely fish", always the anthropomorphic tendency to assign a gender to each fish. Others comment on how it must wish it had never taken my bait and how it must be rueing its luck, but I see it, truly see it: one continuous silver streak of instinct and speed and death and evolutionary beauty. Tight, muscular and ready to take flight at a moment's hesitation or the slightest mistake on my part, this is a raptor of the sea. The fish is tenderly cradled into the water then released to flash back into the depths with a mercurial flick of its tail.

This is no longer any place for us. Ours is a different world, a sparsely populated outpost, not this booming cosmopolis. We decide that now is a good time to leave, packing away quickly and leaving as quietly as we came. I imagine those left on the pier, throwing the occasional curious look in our direction as we shrink and disappear like a mirage into the wavering middle distance, growing smaller and smaller so that, after only a couple of minutes, it seems that we were never there at all.

Day tickets and Daydreams

"I have laid aside business and gone a-fishing."

- *Izaak Walton*

It's well past the hottest part of the day and now I'm relaxing in the comfortable residual warmth of early evening. Shadows loosen and pool all around me like spilled coffee, turning the water under the bankside vegetation black as polished obsidian. Minute by minute the grass cools pleasantly around me, my prone body trapping the last pocket of the day's heat beneath. The only thing disturbing the stillness is a busy haze of midges befuddling the air a couple of feet away.

The two maggots, impaled on my size fourteen hook, wriggle and wave enticingly as they are gently swung out to land with a *plip* just a few yards in front of the bank. The waggler bobs gently then slides into place, becoming no more than a yellow pinpoint in its surroundings.

The float dibs once, twice, then slinks languorously out of sight as something makes contact through the stillness. For a second, I am slow to react. Having anything move in such a perfectly still scene seems almost like accepting that a painting can come to life, so perhaps my mind at first refuses to believe that the float has disappeared. After a second it wakes up to its own error and I lift the rod in a belated response. Luckily, the fish is still there, and I instantly meet solid resistance. It's nothing big – I can tell by the distinct lack of that deep, solid thud-thud that a big fish will send juddering through the shoulder; instead, the sharp, determined rap-rap-rap of something far less grand thrills through my fingers. A few little flicks and plips later and a fin perfect golden rudd is pitched into the landing net, a shiny new pound coin diddering in the bottom of a busker's hat.

I lift it out, marvelling at this little piece of perfection. How nature can create something so beautiful is always beyond me. The closest comparison to having a rudd in the hand that comes to mind from all the centuries of human achievement is a burnished ingot of Aztec gold, but even this image doesn't even begin to come close. No gold, with its dead sheen, can come close to the living brilliance of even a small rudd, and I can't resist one last lingering look as, twisting slightly in my grip, it takes on the running form of the sunset above me, before slipping silently back through my fingers and into the lake.

This was the image I had been feebly grasping at. No, grasping is not the correct verb. Windmilling; mentally I was windmilling at this scene the way a starving man might flail at a limp sandwich suspended on a length of twine six feet above his head. If I could hold onto it for just a minute longer it might help to justify the bloody-minded idiocy in which I had literally found myself ankle deep at that moment.

So, the story begins. Well, actually, it begins at the end of the previous academic year and, to some degree, the end of every other academic year stretching back through living memory.

As the end of the school summer term looms, fetching with it the tantalising prospect of six weeks free of the constraints of timetabled days, balancing equations and grammatical rules and regulations, a mysterious plague sweeps through the schoolchildren of the nation. Sudden fits of strange new never-before-heard-of illnesses tragically strike down a large number of eleven to fifteen-year olds, rendering them unable to drag themselves from their sick beds to attend the lessons they so love.

A few years back, the thought of these poor little mites, pale and shivering beneath their blankets, became too much to bear so, in response to their plight, the school in which I teach introduced an end of year activities week in an effort to heal the town's children and, incidentally, raise end-of-year attendance rates.

For a parental contribution of a few measly pounds, the children could participate in almost anything from mountain biking, swimming and even paintballing, the main idea being to drag their wide, bloodshot-eyed semi-corpses kicking and screaming back from the drooling land of the xbox zombies, and to help them become more active in the fresh air. Nothing clears up a nasty mystery illness like a blast of fresh air.

So, what has this to do with the saccharin-sickly daydream, you might ask? Well, someone happened to whisper around the fact that I enjoy a spot of fishing, one thing led to another and so it came to be that a day of angling on a local coarse fishery was pencilled into the itinerary. *Getting paid to fish? That must be paradise!* I hear you say. Trust me, when I discover exactly who it was that let slip about my piscatorial activities, I'll be acquainting them with the heavy end of my priest. As I watched the teacher in charge of the event pencil my name down letter by letter, *S* - each one – *I* – sounded out – *M* – a hammer stroke – *O* – of impending – *N* – doom. A touch hyperbolic maybe, but I was convinced that the other staff were sniggering and pointing out the individual beads of perspiration forming across my brow as my thoughts drifted toward a dozen kids let loose on a lakeside, on my watch.

I'm a sea angler by trade. Mine is a world of frothing surf lines and big hooks loaded with substantial baits cast way out into the tide, not one of quiet backwaters, gossamer line and dainty morsels.

Before I began sea fishing, I did actually spend one entire summer on my local lake catching the beautifully gilded rudd that had inhabited my recent daydream. My most enduring memory of this is catching a lovely fish of around a pound and a half and, as all children do with their first significant fish, I wanted to take it home to parade in front of all and sundry. In fact, had it been able to survive out of water, I'm sure that I would have attempted to strap a saddle across its back and ride it home in a shower of glory.

As it happened though, the rudd turned out not to be the most successful of land creatures, flipping off its mortal coil after a while, so I took it home with the intention of eating it, (I can practically hear the screams of dismay and anger from the purists winging their way toward me as I write. What can I say? I was kid, revelling in my newfound hunter-gatherer glory) and so, that day, I 'enjoyed' my first and last meal of rudd.

To be fair, my grandmother humoured me with infinite patience and good grace as I forced down each bony mouthful, all the while trying my hardest not to vomit all over her new rug. I quickly came to appreciate the true value of the rudd in its natural environment.

Since that time, I can count on one hand the number of occasions on which I've fished in freshwater, so it now occurred to me that without, perhaps, the exception of applying for a position as one of the Chippendales, never would I be so vastly under qualified for any undertaking as I would be when taking a group of kids to a coarse fishery. But take them I would.

And so there I was, still dressed in shirt and tie from work, like some big, sweaty shire horse turning over the grass patch in my garden whilst watching my golden vision blur away through the sweat running in sticky fingers down my forehead and into my eyes.

When I say a grass patch, I mean exactly that – a patch of grass. Not a lawn, not a strip; a patch. No more than a rough trapezoid of seven feet or so in length. Most who see it would barely consider it worthy of the effort, but somehow it has always played a part in our lives. It has been many things over the years, from soft area to provide a natural cushion beneath our daughter's paddling pool, to a place to simply sit, read and enjoy my pre-work coffee of a summer morning. At the very least it helps to break up the concrete and tarmac monotony of our street, alleviating the blacks and greys with a few blades of green. This time, however, against my better judgement and the knowledge of hours of work ahead to rectify the damage, it was turned into a boggy worm farm.

Within the first couple of shovelfuls, it began: a small wedge of porcelain, a willowy blue pattern printed onto its surface. Was it a plate? I wondered, thinking of someone years ago, sitting down to eat a simple meal from its surface, perhaps bread and cheese, maybe even after doing exactly what I'm doing now. Next came a button, large and black and hard, Bakelite perhaps, its size drawing mental images of oversized woollen cardigans, though the possibilities were almost endless. It made me think of the button-jar my mother kept when we were kids, there for those last-minute emergency repairs, when a near-match or a slight colour variation was permissible, long before the uniformity and stringent perfection of our rampant throwaway modern culture.

The Button-Jar

Such variation is no luxury,
never treat it as such.

Wonderful things should exist
beyond the petty trivia
of those games played at fêtes
in which you have to guess their number
or collective weight.

More appropriate was the exercise
laid down by our English teacher:
'Next lesson, bring a button, any button,
And we'll build a life around it
paragraph by paragraph'
which I did, no difficult task
given the medley in my mother's jar
and the time I'd spend mulling them,

reaching in to hold a fistful for a second
before it slackened and tipped
like rain through my fingers;
a multi-coloured cascade of shapes and sizes
connected only by their four open spaces,
dead centre, regular as compass points or seasons,
all the things we might use to plot a journey
across those wonky, tumbledown inclines
balanced against the sleek glass sides,
sloping upward to one small, bright foothold.

Down I dug, and the objects kept coming, so that it seemed almost like digging down into some ancient well site and lifting out votive offerings – a key; a number of coins both old and new.

A slight move to the right continued to turn up these little curios - a clothes peg, a small rubber bouncy ball and a little plastic toy figure, until I realised with a start that I actually recognised these last few things. The toys belonged to my daughter, no doubt left out at the end of a day's play only to sink down slowly into the earth. The peg was one of a set we were last using regularly five or six years ago, recognisable by its colourful plastic design, and no doubt pinged down to the grass from its tenuous grip on a towel or a bed sheet on some breezy summer's day long since passed. *It's already begun, then*, I thought. Earlier than I thought we might, we were already becoming our own history.

I continued to dig. But why all this effort? Even though I would be fishing carefully manicured lakes, the wilder element in me still clung stubbornly to the untameable. Searching desperately for any vestigial link with the sea, I become fixated upon one fish: the perch. Perhaps it was a throwback to my coarse roots, the bristling have-a-go likeness to the bass or even just the olive and black jungle wildness of its colour scheme that attracted me. Whatever it was, through the twenty years I have been wetting a line, and all the hundreds of monthly angling periodicals I have read, the perch has been one of the few fish that has lodged itself firmly in my thoughts, its tiger stripes searing into my imagination.

I have actually caught a perch some time ago. Bored with the endless tedium of taking roach after roach on feeder and float tactics, I decided to regress to boyhood (can any angler really ever claim to have actually grown up?) and tie a hook, via a three-foot length of mono, onto a gnarled old stick laying at hand, dropping this very basic rig down alongside the bank in front of me.

Within seconds, a fin-perfect three-ounce perch was in my hand and I immediately thought that I'd never seen anything quite so glorious in my life. A beautiful miniature that, despite its predicament, seemed to stare me out as though saying *Come down here, longshanks, and I'll chew yer face off.* Ever since that moment I've hankered after a big perch, an obsession which, in a roundabout way, explains my current predicament. I have decided that, if I must endure the torment that awaits me, I might as well take a pot of lobworms with me and at least give myself a fighting chance of fulfilling my long-held dream at the same time.

Which was all very well and good, but in the meantime, my good lady returned home and began surveying the carnage.

This was frightening.

Shouting I could put up with, threats even, but she stood there, silently shaking her head, scanning back and forth over the crater with the look of a cod that has just been smacked around the head. I think she was probably looking for shards of shrapnel, survivors or any other evidence of the bomb that must have caused this muddy chaos.

I decided that I may be in trouble, so thought it best not to speak. Ever again.

One sweat-grimed hour, a garden that would take three weeks to put back together, and a look frosty enough to chill an eskimo's whatsits later, I had eight worms. Eight. This had better be worth it.

*

The big day dawned clear and cloudless and, despite the events of the previous day, I found myself in a surprisingly buoyant mood. I arrived at school for half past eight where the group of intrepid would-be piscators stood waiting in a kind of ramshackle parade, their motley array of cobbled-together tackle, much of which looked like it hadn't seen the light of day for at least a few years, making me smile at the memory of my own early fishing days. A few pairs of wellies and a dozen carrier bags filled with sandwiches and pop were loaded onto the minibus and we were on our way with no problems. Everyone here? Everyone buckled up? So far so good.

It was only when we were halfway to our destination that one of the boys (let us refer to him for now as *Bobo*. It just seems to fit, as you'll discover) sidled forward.

"Sir."

"Yes, Bobo?"

"What do you reckon to these, sir? Think I'll catch a load of fish using these?" at which point he produced a large box of hand tied flies in and endless combination of colours, sizes and opalescent tints.

"They won't be any good to you today, Bobo. We're going to a coarse fishery; there's no fly fishing there."

"Oh."

Although I'm no fly fisherman, even I could see that this was an impressive collection, so how a young lad had come to be in possession of at least two hundred hand-tied flies was making me extremely curious. "Where did you get them, Bobo?"

"My mother gave them to me to bring. They belonged to her first husband. He died."

That lightened the mood nicely.

At this point I looked over Bobo's shoulder and noticed that, on our day trip to what is regarded as one of the finest coarse fisheries in Wales, he had come armed with a twelve foot, four to eight-ounce rated beachcaster that probably possessed enough grunt to relieve a whale of its spine. My mood began to resemble the last balloon left at the party – lifeless, limp and draped pathetically over my shoulder.

It was going to be a long day.

*

We arrived at our destination without further incident and, to be fair, it did make a pretty impressive sight. From our high vantage point in the car park we had a panoramic view down over much of the six-acre expanse of the fishery, with its numerous small lakes spread out before us, looking like pools of chocolate after the recent rain. To our right stood a series of log cabins built for the serious carpers who come to spend weekends and, occasionally, even weeks here.

It was a striking place alright, and many of the ingredients were there for any nature lover – an abundance of overgrown flora bursting with life and colour, dragonflies sparking in and out of the margins, kingfishers perched amongst the reeds and even a buzzard, working the sky in its long, lazy loops over one of the further lakes.

But something didn't quite sit right.

It wasn't simply the fact that this was a coarse fishing venue. I love sea fishing but could often happily picture myself wasting a few hours beside some overhung, trilling stretch of the Wye, Avon or Stour, but when it comes to these commercial fisheries, I can't seem to get past the fact that all of this is man-made, a created fantasy borne of the designs of one man rather than a series of interlinking natural processes.

Let me put it another way. Imagine, if you will, that some panel of cultural gurus had commissioned Botticelli to depict, in paint, the perfect woman, a woman so gloriously stunning that she would make Venus croak like a jealous old crone and stagger off her shell. He paints with love and painstakingly laborious care, lavishing her with a master's focus so that, when gazing at the painting, your brain is tricked into believing that this is more than it seems to be: this is art made flesh – the eye can't help but linger a moment too long upon a pair of smooth legs, running over milky thighs and up to the exquisitely feminine curves of the torso that catch the light like polished alabaster. At this point, though, you discover that somewhere along the line, old Botticelli has been given his marching orders and they've drafted in Picasso to finish off the head. Interesting, yes, but something doesn't quite gel, the elements don't fit together. This, in a nutshell, is how I feel about commercial coarse fisheries.

"What are you fancying today, mate?" my colleague Steve asked. My last experience of coarse fishing had been a decade before, and then it had only been roach fishing under a waggler, so I was deferring to his greater experience.

"I don't mind mate," I replied. "As long as there's a bend in the rod."

We descended en masse upon the office to pay and check in, the boys buzzing excitedly around us like something out of *The Lord of the Flies*. Each of us paid in turn and walked away with a free pot of maggots that would be of little use if we were to feeder fish here, the fish displaying a preference for sweetcorn and small boilies.

Glancing at the map of the venue while strolling in to the

office, we had spied a small lake tucked away at the back of the fishery, in a neglected corner far from the more popular specimen and match lakes, ignored for these more appealing, better stocked lakes closer to the amenities. Passing a few anglers on the way down, we made enquiries as to what could be caught in this lake, picking up replies like 'Bits' and 'A few F1s.' Now, I'm no snob, but the thought of fishing for something that fell off the back of an algebraic formula left me feeling somewhat cold until Steve hissed in my direction "They're carp, mate", which immediately perked me up no end.

Now here was something I can work with, a target I can really get my teeth into, as I had never before caught a carp. Ah well, if the perch didn't fancy it at least I had a back-up plan.

I trundled on with the blind faith of a pilgrim, determined to find the perch swim I knew was waiting for me somewhere out there. After a short time, and to my utter amazement, I found it, and it was perfect, just as it had been in my imaginings. To my left lay a shaded corner wearing a patchwork quilt of leaves and dappled by the shade of an alder, with a small bed of lily pads just beyond; right in front of me, about twenty yards away, lay a couple of small overgrown islands that were densely populated with reeds and grasses. If there were predators about, then surely this was where I was going to find them.

The main problem with this swim, however, was that it was, quite literally, a dump. Either there was a small herd of deer roaming the grounds nearby or the angler who had used this swim before me had very innovatively tried to break the monotony of a fishless session by conducting their own *poop-a-thon*. The swim was littered, nay, festooned, in faeces of all the various natural (and some quite unnatural) shades of brown. I hadn't brought any form of seatbox as I had decided to travel light, carrying my gear in a rucksack. On the balance of things though, the swim really was too good to turn up, so I decided to take my chances, pulling up and unloading my gear at Crap Central.

With trembling fingers, I threaded the line through the rings, setting up a basic feeder rig, planning to offer up a bed of wriggling fat maggots on which to lay my worms. Despite my misgivings I was almost at the point of contributing to the poop-a-thon with excitement as I reached into my bag…and discovered that my worms, all eight of them, were still wriggling around in lively pristine condition. The main problem with this was that they were still in my fridge. Right, compose yourself. Not to worry; I also had a full half pint pot of maggots, enough to tempt any self-respecting perch within casting distance.

I cast in, landing the rig no more than twelve inches from the first of the small islands and, with a little air punch, settled back into the session. As always, the urgency and tension that builds up before the first cast washes away the moment it's in the water. The building heat of the morning and the gentle buzz of the flies lulled me immediately into a semi-doze so that the half breeze block I'd salvaged for a seat was digging into my backside began to creak with the soft give of a wicker creel underneath me and Bobo, now attired in tank top and short trousers, hair carefully brylcreemed into a middle parting, materialised at my feet, gazing up awestruck at a master at work.

"Now watch carefully young Bobo, and you too may one day master such a noble adversary."

"Gosh! Do you really think so, Sir? Could it possibly be?"

"Maybe lad, maybe."

At this, my split cane rod hooped over, the reel screamed out in alarm and I resolutely tucked my pipe into the corner of my mouth (luckily, the tweed jacket with leather elbow patches is neatly folded beside me, leaving my arms, shirtsleeves rolled up, free) in readiness for the fight ahead.

"By golly, it's a big one, it's magnificent, it's…"

I never got to see that fish because at that precise moment, the voice of the real Bobo shredded the air, making mincemeat of the tranquil atmosphere and this fragile dream-image.

"Sir! Siiiiiiiiiiirrrrr!!!!"

"Eh? Wha..? What is it, Bobo?" I asked, casually flicking another turd from my sandwich.

"I fell in!"

There was no need to explain. As he waddled around the lake toward me, I could see that everything from the nipples down was now a uniform shade of grey-brown. Amazing; we'd only been at the place for twenty minutes, were miles from the sea, and still he had managed to establish his own high tide mark.

With a flourish, Bobo stated the obvious – "I don't think I like fishing, Sir", and with that, promptly trundled into my pot of maggots, launching it into a beautiful parabolic arc to land six or seven feet behind me, minus the contents which instantly begin to attract the attention of the sparrows. Oblivious to what he and his meaty trotters had done, Bobo then flumped down on his back next to me, resembling a mortally wounded starfish. I hadn't the heart to point out that he was lying in a latrine.

Okay, carp it was then.

*

After making sure that the pupils were set up with various float and feeder rigs, I set up an open-ended feeder rig and started to bait the swim, repeatedly casting feederfuls of hemp, crushed pellet and corn. Watching all of this was Beth, a young, timid year seven pupil who had kept herself apart from the rest of the group.

"You okay, Beth?"

"Yes sir."

"Would you like me to set up a rod for you?"

"No thank you, sir. I'll just watch."

Try as I may, Beth couldn't be persuaded to take a rod, choosing instead to sit on the bank and watch as I fished on.

An hour later, and finally the fuss had died down. All was peaceful with the world aside from the gentle plashes of kingfishers at work and the soft reverberations of Bobo's snores threading the air.

The quiver tip, inactive for so long, had begun to gently merge into the background in the way that something that does not fulfil its only intended use will become just another part of the scenery, like dusty tools hung in the shed, or neglected cooking implements on the kitchen worktop of a takeaway addict.

Dink. Dink. The tip tapped over twice and was suddenly wrenched free of its surroundings, rocketing once more into the foreground of my vision.

Dink. Dink. DINK! The tip slammed over, stayed over, and instantly I swept the rod sideways until it hooped and locked down, causing the reel's lightly set clutch to offer up half a yard of line with a satisfying, crotchety groan, making it immediately obvious that this was a half - decent fish.

The line planed back and forth under the water in a dogged but straightforward fight. Leading up to today, I had been preparing myself to hook into a jagged juggernaut that would slice the lake, bass-like, and fight me like some squat, angry, veteran boxer, but this fish was just…well…loping. To be fair, it did take line against the clutch, but after two minutes of fighting, my first ever carp slid over the net, its two-tone flanks relaxing into the grass like buttered toffee in the early light. Okay, it wasn't a perch, but I still felt absolutely ecstatic. That first experience of anything in angling is always still the best feeling in the world, and one of its most effective opiates, driving the angler straight back for more. With trembling fingers, I quickly rebaited and recast, eager to get back amongst the fish. The rig plopped over the same spot and settled into the rest.

Within two minutes the rod hooped over again. YES! Again, I struck into the fish, it took line against the lightly set drag and after two minutes it slipped over the lip of the net looking like buttered to…hang on a minute…This looked like exactly the same fish. Maybe it was. How the bloody hell was I supposed to tell?!

Right. Hang on. Gently cradling the fish, I walked a few swims down the lake, about fifty yards in all, before releasing the fish then trotting back to my swim to rebait and recast back over the bait bed.

I didn't have a chance to sit back down before I was connected to another fish, all tussle and shoulder, that scrapped away, zigging and zagging back and forth before slipping over the net like bu…oh, sod it. This was getting stupid now.

Just as I was pondering my way out of this hall of mirrors, I heard a *plip* followed by a fit of giggling; another *plip* and more giggling. I looked down to see Beth staring down into the water just out beyond the margins as it erupted once more to the surface - sucking action of a mob of tiny mouths. Some of the maggots so gracefully hoofed from their pot by Bobo earlier had managed to evade the attentions of the local bird life and wriggled their way to the edge of the bank, only to squirm into those waiting mouths.

Picking up a nearby stick, I tied off two feet of six-pound monofilament, all that I had lying around, to the smallest hook I could find, baited it with a stray maggot picked out of the grass and handed it to Beth.

"Go on then."

"What? Me, sir? What do I do?" She resembled a tiny woodland creature that had just stumbled onto an A-road and become aware that it was about to become roadkill.

"Just lower it into the water slowly." Gently, she lowered the baited hook and almost instantaneously was plugged into something, the shock jolting up her arm.

"Woah! What do I do?!" Her face flickered like a faulty computer monitor, her thoughts as frozen as a crashed website, stuck somewhere between utter panic and sheer joy.

"You just..." but already my words were redundant as that hidden instinct, there somewhere in all of us, kicked in, and she flipped a tiny fish into her palm with another of those little giggles. A perch.

As I looked down at the tiny fish in Beth's palm, my own dream perch turned away and began to merge back into the silty depths of my imagination. That's the funny thing about dreams like this. We develop an almost parental relationship with them – they are delivered to us suddenly one day, and we can do nothing but nurture them, watch them grow and develop and change over the years until they come to form a central part of our lives. And maybe, after all those long years, some of us achieve these dreams, catch the fish that we have loved and felt haunted by for all that time, and some of us have to watch as others achieve them in our place until one day, perhaps one day...

I looked around me and saw the same thing waiting to happen in some of the members of this small group, all of whom I'd known since they were trembling, petrified eleven-year olds in a uniform too big for them. In a few short months some of them would seem suddenly taller, voices a shade deeper, and in their swagger an increased confidence and hunger for the great wide world, ready to march out, chattering, through the doors for the last time in search of long-imagined futures of their own.

Somewhere on the bank behind us, the feeder rod, idle in the rest, sank slowly back into its surroundings again. Just before we had to wake Bobo there would be time for a few more. We impaled another maggot on the hook and began to lower it down into the margins, our blurry faces wobbling in the sunlit water as another host of tiny mouths rose to meet them.

The Sunbird

As I stepped out through the back door into my garden, I was greeted by an unseasonal flurry of white.

"You might want to check your border there" my neighbour Lynne called over the garden wall. "A bird's just been taken".

The neighbour's privet overhangs the wall, and thrums throughout the summer with the fuss and chatter of sparrows, warblers and whitethroats, especially on our side, which I often leave in a slightly unruly state purely to attract the little birds and their evening music. Tonight, the chorus would be one voice lighter.

I never saw the killer, but the sparrow hawk suddenly burst back into my mind, resurrected by Lynne's words to shred that fine line between memory and actuality with renewed purpose, as I pictured it swooping low and clamping onto its victim. Only a week previously, those piercing gold eyes had fixed upon me, running me through over and over. I stumbled on it by fluke, ambling through the back door with a cup of tea. My clumsy, surprised gawp followed its own unmoving, awkward line while the sparrow hawk never stopped moving, fending my gaze with constant small, sharp adjustments of its head, much like an experienced fencer flicking the wrist almost imperceptibly to throw their opponent off balance and score a hit time and time again.

Aside from its head, everything else remained stock still, the inverted V of the shed roof inert like a downed thrush beneath its talons, the garden neatly halving itself along the raptor's razor-line of sight. Then, with casual disdain it tore itself loose, took to the air and shook of the earth, leaving me static in its slipstream. In no time it was just a speck moving away over the hills from which it had likely come.

There were a few tiny spots of blood spattered across the leaves of the fuchsia, but no more. I started a quick search, scrabbling with my fingertips, riffling through the lavender and rooting about beneath the roses, but too late. All the fuss had attracted the attentions of Elle.

"What are you looking for, Daddy?" she asked, as I searched. What could I say? Here I was, desperately trying to make sure that there was no evidence of the attack, trying, in my own fumbling way, to protect her by making sure that she didn't stumble across some tiny ball of wreckage.

"Er…just checking for something, love" I replied, not convincing her in the slightest. Still I kept looking, wondering whether all this was actually for her benefit or for mine, and all the while those downy fathers kept

falling

  falling

    falling.

Come on, love. Let's go and finish packing. Looking back over my shoulder, I guided her back inside as the last of the feathers settled to the ground.

Three hours and a few re-packed cases later, we were ready to go.

"Got everything? Phone? Wallet? Keys?"

"Yes, yes. Don't fuss! I've got everything!" We bustled and chinked and thudded our way around the car, ensuring everything was packed away. After months of waiting, at the end of a long and very tiresome academic year, the summer break had finally arrived, yet even now, with our holiday within our grasp, leaving for Tenby was so typical of life – getting in the way, unwilling to release us into something simpler.

"Right. All ready? Let's g…"

"Have you packed your fishing gear?"

"I…" quite clearly hadn't packed the fishing gear, and quite clearly should have listened to my wife earlier, or so her look told me. Five minutes later, the rucksack, travel rod and collapsible sand spike were packed in the boot and we were finally ready.

Because my wife had been working until nine, we would be making the journey as the evening wore down. We hit the motorway as the gloaming began to envelop us, but despite the early advances of night there was an overwhelming sense of release in the car. The further west we travelled the less influence our daily lives seemed to exert. Everything began to thin out, from lights to buildings to people; the world was decluttering itself around us as we watched, driving further into, yet farther from, existence as we knew it.

Above the industrial skyline of my home town the sunsets are always fiery, decked out in their reds and oranges and yellows as though burning back at their setting, raging in response. But on our westward tack, there was none of this. We had cleared the established industrial borders of Port Talbot, Neath and Swansea and were greeted with a day ending in far more contemplative hues – blues, jades, greens, gently washing out like an ebbing tide retreating gently from tidal sand channels.

Driving west, moving away from the deeper influences of industry, the agricultural expanses of west Wales began to open up before us, the patchwork of rural villages dotting the landscape. Many of them were small, barely glimpsed in the distance or flashing here and there between trees and service stations, the presence of some of them given away only by a spire standing proud, as though marking where some great peg had been driven into the earth to prevent these little communities from flapping away.

*

Already, the day had become hot. Having arrived in a fluster of bags and bits and bobs, we had simply unloaded everything into my uncle's caravan, grabbed a bite to eat and crashed out to sleep. Waking in a fug the morning after, we decided that the clothes could be taken care of at another point in the day, and so, after breakfast, decided to go in search of something a little more serene.

Come to a different world

said the placard on the harbour-side ticket booth,

An Island of Peace, Tranquillity and Unspoilt Natural Beauty.

The boat trip to the monastic island of Caldey seemed exactly what we were looking for, so we decided to set off in search of our own small portion. Following the minor stampede for the ticket queue, all those ready to take the boat over to the island were already on the beach. The next boat puttered up alongside the rickety wooden pontoon as we arrived and immediately we, a handful of the estimated sixty thousand tourists received by the island per year, began to clamber aboard.

"Ladies and Gentlemen…" blared the small speaker mounted at the rear of the cabin, "…the journey to the island should take around twenty minutes. We are fully equipped with lifebelts and maintain a constant link with the shore at all times." It seemed that even now, the mainland was reluctant to let us go. Finally, the engine revved with more strength and the little boat tugged free, ploughing its tiny furrow out into the bay.

We hadn't hit open water yet and already I was nervous.

"Be careful there, love"

"It's okay dad, I'm fine!"

Elle carried on twisting and turning and doing her best to take everything in, and it was only with difficulty that I managed to tear my eyes away from her.

"She really will be fine you know," Rachel mumbled. "Try to relax; you'll give yourself an aneurism!"

To take my mind off the lingering presence of danger I began people-watching (and listening) to pass the short journey over to the island. At one extreme, the group of young people who clambered aboard in their green tee-shirts, the word CREW emblazoned across the back, staying true to the stereotype of impatient youth hired in as the part-time summer help, combining the tired or hung-over, head-in-hands semi-sleeping pose with text messaging, tales of last night's antics and bass-heavy dance music thudding through their headphones.

This segued into all the usual touristy chatter about caravans, bed-and-breakfasts and the price of a meal, before faltering and coming to a tremulous slowness on one person. This teenaged youth – quiet, unassuming – sat talking to one of the older members of staff. It seemed that he was considering a monastic vocation and was visiting to stay with the monks in order to make a decision. Such quiet certainty and assuredness flashed across his face that, as we approached the island and I watched the seabirds flap and flail around us, I found myself somewhat envious – twice his age, and feeling as though I had less than half a clue as to how to go about life.

The day approached lunchtime and grew hot. The boats had been steadily disgorging day-trippers for two hours and the village green had become crowded, as had the usual destinations - the chocolate factory, the gift shops and the tearoom. For many, it seemed that the purpose of the island held no significance, so the churches remained quiet, even the Abbey church itself. Looking at the sign outside the door, it appeared that Sext was due to begin in twenty minutes, so we climbed the short staircase to the gallery and took a seat in the burgeoning silence.

Looking down, I was struck by the austerity of the place, although austerity seems to be rather a harsh noun with which to label the building's simple, effective beauty, the same beauty that is to be found in a machine purely engineered and stripped back to its serious, and very specific, purpose. Every single plain line and quiet corner of the layout, each sparse element of decoration, bore plain testament to a long tradition of introspection. Like a blank page the bare walls and ever circling routines drive its inhabitants deeper and deeper into the experiences and truths of their lives on the island. Day after day the celebrants are greeted with a fresh balance sheet, a zeroed tally in their plain walls, their simple altar, their hardwood stalls, and themselves.

Aside from the signs exhorting THIS IS A SILENT AREA,

the nature of the atmosphere itself seems fabricated from that same silence; I felt like I could hang any of my thoughts on upon it for as long as I needed, but what then? If the faith of these men were one vast, silent room, my thoughts would only take up a handful of pegs. I doubted that I would ever have enough faith or prayers to fill even a corner of that room, but with doubt, I might. Maybe, I thought, that's the point. Maybe they, like me, have the doubt to fill this place, with the only difference being that they were more equipped with the spiritual articulacy to declare, and begin to deal with, that doubt.

Others had started to fill the gallery, the rustling of rucksacks and waterproof jackets crinkling the air's smooth surface. Despite the signs and the fact that the service was soon to begin, many of them were chatting and peering around, their whispering reverberating from wall to wall in a theatrical manner as they wandered to the edge of the gallery to crane over and get a better look at the monks' stalls. Having arrived early, I was settled in the front row. In contrast to the noisy newcomers, someone was already praying in the pew next to me.

Then, the pealing of bells. The short service began in a sonorous wave of plainchant:

In the name of the Fa-ther and of the Son and of the Holy Spi-rit

There were those among us who are immediately stilled into silence, yet there were still those who were fidgeting and whispering despite the solemnity of the moment.

The Lord of the Hosts is with us

The prayers continued from the woman on my right as the monks got into full flow

The God of Jacob is my strong-hold.

Wave upon wave of soft vocals rolled on and flowed over us

all yet still there were those who left halfway through or continued to chatter, totally segregated from what was happening around them while others were rooted to the spot, totally entranced as the chant began to wind down

As it was in the beginning, is now and ever shall be...

And the silence began its shadow-slow creeping back in around the edges

World without end...

and the whole room seemed to exhale

Amen.

Their devotions over, the monks began to filter out, again bowing low as they passed the altar before gently swishing out of church. The seats emptied as the small crowd ebbed away, leaving just the three of us to digest what we had seen and heard, to spend time in the company of our own thoughts once more.

Afterward, stepping from the coolness of the church into the midday heat was something of a shock, a fact not helped by the masses of tourists regurgitated onto the jetty by the successive boats that had been endlessly looping back and forth from the mainland. Tired of so much bustle, we headed away from the tourists' focal point, leaving them to the gift shop, café and small museum, heading back past the Abbey itself which, in the high summer light, had the pure lime-washed shine of an Italian villa or a fortification perched atop a Greek cliff.

Bearing right, leaving the last of the tourists at the chocolate factory, we arrived at the medieval priory buildings, standing quiet, aloof. They had seen it all, from the comings and goings of the Normans, the Dissolution, to the conversion back to Rome in the early 20th century.

The second oldest Roman Catholic church used for worship in England and Wales, although it had received a recent facelift, had its wiring spruced up and a lick of paint, it appeared to retain much of its age in the fabric of its construction. The beautiful cobbled floor, worn smooth by years of footfalls, sifted the sounds of our steps into a soft shuffle and the dark, varnished wood of the meagre stalls seemed to suck the light into its grain, leaving the place with the dimness I always imagined harboured by such churches of the Middle Ages.

Moving forward toward the altar, something caught my eye as it fluttered on the surface, lifting then falling. On the altar itself lay numerous thin slips of paper. On closer inspection, I realised that they were small prayers for loved ones now departed, medical problems, family ties, relationships, jobs and dozens of other small petitions left here in the hope that they might rise up and be fulfilled.

We wrote our own prayers; mine, as always, for my family:

Lord, watch over my family, keep my daughter from harm...

and placed them upon the altar. Suddenly, our eyes were drawn again, this time to the eaves, as small, dark shapes flitted in and out of the spaces between beams. As our eyes adjusted to the dark of the roof space, we made out a rag-tag assortment of bundled mud, straw and fluff and the swallows arrowing in and out of them. It appeared that they had come to settle here, attracted perhaps by the spirit of the island's own version of a St. Kevin or St. Francis. Beautiful and direct, they never seemed to congregate here for long, darting out through the doors as we watched, fluttering then lifting quickly out of sight.

*

Back on the mainland later that evening, we headed to the beach for a quiet couple of hours, allowing me the chance to break out the fishing gear.

Even here in this holiday destination, surrounded by scenes of relaxation, there were signs of the world's tendency to move on quickly, not lingering anywhere for too long. As we walked onto the sand, a ring of five disposable barbecues lay carelessly abandoned where they were used at some point late last night; already they looked like some kind of black and grey fossilized remains of summer enjoyment long forgotten. Elle darted around my feet – "I'm going to make a sandcastle, daddy" and "Can I bury you, daddy?" or "I'm really looking forward to swimming, daddy!"

Leaving Rachel and Elle to lay our stuff on the sand at the high tide line, I wandered down to the waterline to get set up, clipping on a simple single-hook rig, baiting up with a strip of mackerel and clipping the whole lot down. There was no question of swinging a lead, so I laid the whole lot back in a straight line behind me and used the length of the rod to ping it safely away in a straight line over my head, landing it seventy yards or so away from where I stood.

The evening began to wind down, the numbers of people around me thinning out a little as they headed back to their holiday lets and caravans, or into town in search of a quiet drink or two. The last of the mackerel boats puttered back in from the bay, ready to drop their final loads of sunburnt, happy holidaymakers with their strings of mackerel. Those few left on the beach began lighting their barbecues as the air continued to cool and lose the sweaty clinginess of the earlier hours of the day.

"Daddy!" Elle flustered down the beach toward me. "Daddy, have you caught anything yet?"

"No." Although she didn't show any, I felt the disappointment for her, having hoped all along that a stray dogfish might wander along and impale itself just to add a little excitement to her day. She's Daddy's girl alright. I remember myself at her age – elbow deep in muck and crawling with bugs, and yet as I looked down into her eyes, I couldn't help but feel the pangs of wanting to keep her forever wrapped in cotton wool.

"Can I have a go?"

"Of course you can, love!" I stood her in front of me and fidgeted around her, altering her stance, holding the rod with her, going over the instructions one more time: "Keep your arms apart…careful not to catch you hand on the reel there…"

"Okay, okay, don't fuss me Daddy!" She was raring to go.

"Okay love, here we go. Look up, bring your left hand down and follow through with your right…" the lead flew away cleanly to thirty yards. Elle looked thunderstruck, an expression of shock slowly giving way to a huge smile that spread gradually across the whole lower half of her face.

"Yaaaay!!!" Rachel cheered from further up the beach. Elle turned to receive the plaudits with a little hop of triumph, starting to raise her arms and, for just a moment I found myself able to take W.H Davies' lead, to stand and stare while my daughter flapped around me in her excitement, like a little sunbird, ready to take flight.

We slept that night to a cacophony of rain: rain blurring the windows, rain hammering at the roof, rain slashing at our exposed faces whenever we opened the door to glance outside. All night it hammered on, battering as though to be let in until finally, at two in the morning, I got up for a moment. I opened the door for some air and the racket of wind in the trees was almost indistinguishable from the roar of the surf carrying from the nearby south beach as it stung my eyes. I locked up again and headed back to bed. Passing my daughter's bedroom door, I paused, ready to go in and check on her one more time. Listening to the gentle chirp of her deep breathing, I thought better of it, instead pulling her door closed and going back to my own bed. As I slowly slid into sleep I thought of that small group across the dark waters who, in an hour's time, would be waking into a new day, lifting their prayers again, calling out to God himself from the pre-dawn shadows.

Guillemot

Auk
as some would have you classified,
as though such exclamation
were enough.

I feel like I could reach
Out and clutch the polished solidity
of your head, your neck,
but then you turn away to preen
and they crumble like charcoal,
leaving your breast empty, unfinished.

And you, sea-bird, sky-bird,
if you don't know what comes next
how could I?

Turning on the Dark

"This is a good one, Elle. Nice and flat."
"Yep. We'll have that one."
"What about this one?"
"Go on then, we'll have that one too."

At some point in the distant past, somewhere miles upstream from our home, the persistent ministrations of frost and rain and heat gradually wore down a seam of rock until, in one final flourish, some landslide crumpled it to earth, shattering it into dozens of smaller rocks. From there, the river picked up the reins and eventually, through flood and flow, saltation and attrition, shifted them all downstream, knapped them smooth and round and rolled them to a standstill just a couple of miles from the sea on a shallow, wide dried-out riverbed, where we were now taking our pick.

Skipping between the rounded pebbles, we scrutinised the various stones for the best specimens, rejecting those that were too spherical or too narrow, sifting through the pock-marked remnants of house-bricks that had also received the river's attention over the months and years, leaving them looking like desiccated sponges, eventually settling on a small carrier bag full that we prepared to cart back to the garden.

The 'AFAN VALLEY ANGLING CLUB. NO CANOEING' sign erected across the river hinted that there are those who don't see this as somewhere merely to pass through, but as somewhere to linger awhile so I took a minute or two before leaving. Looking around, I noticed how much the scene had changed with the recent sun. The same weather that had dropped the river levels and allowed us to come and gather our stones had allowed myriad colonies to spring up like miniature fiefdoms on the small islands dotted here and there: yellow flag iris; daisies; purple loosestrife, all nestling together on their tiny, multicultural

Zanzibars, a sight made all the prettier for the fact that all of this would be swept away in the autumnal spates.

Once home, the real work began. With an almost military precision, my daughter laid out an array of small brushes, paints and a pot of water, then set about transforming them, tongue poking from the corner of her mouth as she dipped then re-dipped the paint brush and brought the watercolour pictures to life one by one – a beach, the house bathed in sunshine and backed by a blue sky, then another of the house surrounded by a night scene, a black sky full of stars.

"What do you think, Dad?"

"Beautiful. Let's leave them to dry."

A few hours later, as I was lifting the gear from the shed ready for the night's fishing, Elle, decked out in her pyjamas, stepped out into the garden to check on her handiwork just as the light was beginning to fail. There they were, dry now and beautiful in their little details. "Look, Dad. The daytime picture was the right one earlier, but now the night time picture's the right one. One for each part of the day!" We both looked up involuntarily but there were no stars yet, only a pale arc of moon that… "What was that, Dad?!" We watched, silently, then there it was again, again now and yet again, slashing over us. The bats were out, and in full hunting mode already. "That, my lovely, is a sign that it's time a certain little someone should be in bed."

*

I've had to slow down as there are no streetlights out in these rural back lanes. Aside from the windows of a few scattered country pubs, the only significant light on this leg of the journey comes from the lamps positioned to illuminate the church of St. Mary Magdalene in the village of Kenfig. Perhaps unnecessary but, in its own way, quite beautiful, there is just enough light to pick out the crenelated tower, balancing itself against the darkness at its base from which it seems to rise like a beacon, often as a staging point on early morning journeys homeward after long and tiring night sessions.

This makes me think of a story I was told recently by someone whose friend had put their son to bed one night, saying "I'm going to turn the light off now, but don't panic because mummy and daddy will be just downstairs", only to be told:

"No daddy, you're turning on the dark."

For twenty minutes the boy's parents waited outside the door, ready for the expected invasion of ghouls and boggarts, but as their son fell asleep, he never made a sound.

The bats are still very active, as they were earlier, swishing in and out of my headlight beams. I don't know what the bat mortality rate is where cars are concerned, so I take my foot off the pedal a touch more. I prefer by far to fish after dark, but in these lighter summer months the available darkness shrinks to a small six-hour strip wedged in between great chunks of daylight, making me like a stickleback in a sun-shrunk pool. I am also very aware that I share this little bit of darkness, hence the decision I made on my new headlamp, which arrived today.

Although it's from a very reputable manufacturer, it's not one of their flagship products. It wasn't a monetary thing that influenced my decision – one of those über-lights would have cost me only around twenty pounds more than the model I plumped for. The reason for my choice was light output – I wanted less of it.

Lighting is one of those areas in which angling, sea angling in particular, has come on in leaps and bounds in recent years. In this, the gilded age of Information Technology, a world in which we are assured and reassured that bigger is always most definitely better, headlamps have been pimped up and souped-up – the norm is currently standing at around two hundred lumens which, when put into perspective, is enough to light up a large portion of the lane behind my house. Browsing the internet recently, I stumbled across a light that claimed an eye-watering light output of nearly two thousand lumens. In our current eco-society much is rightly made of pollution – rubbish in our streets and how to deal with it through recycling, the pollution of our waterways; and the newspaper headlines reflect this accordingly. Even noise pollution occasionally rears its head and stabs its way into the odd page four story of the tabloids. But light pollution seems, in a twist of irony not lost upon me, to remain in the dark.

Plants aside, light is not essential to our survival. If we were to take vitamin D supplements to compensate for the lack of sunlight, we could survive indefinitely without it. There would, of course, be some disruption to our Diel cycle – the natural rhythm between diurnal and nocturnal activity – but this wouldn't prove too much of a problem; just ask those living in the Arctic Circle how they cope with a night that is three months long.

This is, of course, slightly depressing. We need that balance, to know, like that boy in the story I was told, that day will follow night and spring will follow winter, and this is the way it has always been. But thanks to the single-minded obsession with advancement kick-started by the Industrial Revolution, we are suffering from the effects of a three-hundred-year hangover, swinging well past the equilibrium mark and lasering off into the distance. Man said, 'Let there be more light', and it was so.

Apparently, each time I stand out in my garden and look up into the night sky, I am able to see somewhere in the region of two hundred stars. Were I to do the same thing in an open, isolated rural area such as a sizeable country park, if I had the patience to count them all, I wouldn't stop until I reached a number in the thousands. The main hindrance to my doing this, though, is the fact that there are less and less places in which to actually do this.

If we were to drift momentarily into orbit around our own planet, we would truly witness the full extent of our addiction. Where should we go first? Maybe we'll hit the boulevards of Las Vegas, allowing ourselves to float past its strip joints and casinos, our wide eyes transfixed as those of a tiny creature on the tendril of an angler fish. This city in which most of the establishments actually omit the majority of their natural light and contain no clocks in order to prevent gamblers from thinking about the time of day and, therefore, realising they have a life outside gambling, uses billions of candles worth of light every week.

Not to your taste? A little gaudy maybe? Okay, let's try somewhere with a little more low-key glamour. Now we're taking a slightly more leisurely stroll, peering in through side street windows at the faintly dipping candle lights and chiaroscuro ambience of Parisian bistros and cafés, meandering gently down the avenues until we suddenly arrive at the Eiffel tower, its beams reaching out from its tip into the middle of a black infinity as dark as any deep sea ocean trench.

From this viewpoint it quickly becomes obvious that there are few places on earth that serve as the last hiding places of true dark; most of the planet's surface resembling a giant switchboard. In fact, it seems to have become such a problem that some scientists have begun to sit up and take notice, resulting in the International Dark Sky Foundation, an organisation whose mission statement is

"to preserve and protect the night time environment and our heritage of dark skies".

The foundation takes its work very seriously indeed, seeking the true sanctuaries of dimness, setting up protected areas of darkness with heavy controls on lighting. But why go to all this trouble? To this, I would reply: 'Why not?' Sometimes, an answer is not needed; sometimes, the darker it is the clearer things can become.

Even our beaches, so often the dark fringes of our island home, are now under attack. Step onto many beaches now and the signs are already in evidence that a battle is taking place. The reflections of the lights which intersperse the promenades are cast down upon the wet sand, elongated, the natural and the synthetic uneasily merging in the livid orange-yellow scars so that walking down to the surf line can occasionally look like you are kicking through the embers of some huge bonfire.

Even those beaches nowhere near residential areas are under attack, and anglers are the vanguard of this assault. Calling out to a fellow angler during a night session on any local coastline is likely to result in the retinas being scorched from your skull as the full beam casually sweeps across your face.

The lamp I recently purchased, in comparison, has a maximum light output of ninety lumens, as well as two other settings of fifty lumens and a miserly three lumens. What could anyone possibly do with just three lumens of light? It is a well-known fact to anglers that a full moon, hanging high and bright in the sky, can put the fish down or, at the very least, make them very tentative to bite, limiting a close-in bass or sole session to a few skittish plucks on the rod tip at best. It would, therefore, stand to reason that a beam of light resembling the landing of the Starship Enterprise would lead to a blank session.

Rather than taking the fight to the darkness I much prefer to set up a base camp of light and let the dark envelop me. There is nothing quite like the hiss of a petrol or gas lantern, a pie sat on top, warming away. To react to a bite is to step out of the circle of light into the unknown beyond it and to fetch something back out of the blackness, more of a careful salvage operation rather than a full-frontal assault.

When given the proper respect, true darkness can really show its colours. Centuries ago, sailors would stare aghast and fall to their knees in fear and reverential awe as Saint Elmo's Fire clung to the tip of their mast, making it glow like a spectral finger pointing heavenward. When the first primitive exploratory expeditions of mankind struck into the far north, they must have thought the world was coming to an end as they watched Aurora Borealis flicker out across the sky.

Once, I had such an encounter myself, though the circumstances were perhaps less in the tradition of romantic discovery. It had been one of those fantastic August mackerel days, the barometric pressure riding as high as the tide at dusk, and not a breath of wind stirred anywhere. It was one of those days that just seem to come together, peaking at dusk in a striped frenzy.

Everyone had a bag full of fish for the two 'b's – bait and barbecue, and I was relaxing with my grandfather and a neighbour, lounging around and making the odd cast into the sea which, by now, mirrored the black of the sky. We had not planned to stay so long, so had brought no torches, but were compelled to stay by the evening's slow inky slide toward its end.

After maybe half an hour of tea drinking and chatting, I decided to have a few more casts before breaking down my tackle for the night. I leaned back, gave the string of tinsel lures a flick and caught my breath as they hit the water with a luminous plop, flinging droplets of comic book radioactivity everywhere. I had never seen bioluminescence in action before and watched amazed as my line fizzed through the electric water, finally pulling out the string of bright green feathers like a colour-filtered special effect from a sci-fi film.

Looking back, I wish I could say that I spent few moments committing this minor miracle to memory, jotting down my thoughts or maybe even snapping a few pictures as I marvelled in wonder at this lovely natural phenomenon, but I was thirteen years old and didn't have a camera, so…quickly, I propped my rod against a rock, unzipped my fly and peed copiously over the side of the breakwater, chuckling to myself as though watching a display on Bonfire Night, and shouting "Look at this!"

Equally, I wish I could say that the shouts and reprimands of outraged adults floated at me across the air, but a minute later my grandfather, neighbour and a string of other stragglers lined up, faced the water and unleashed the fourth of July.

Would this sudden burst of light have been so appreciated or even noticed, had there been a battery of headlamps and petrol lanterns illuminating the pier? Maybe the joy came from the fact that I had been craving a little illumination all along – looking for the one thing to brighten up that evening, but hadn't realised it until it had, quite literally, splashed up in front of me.

All I know is that now, entering the residential outskirts of Porthcawl, this sudden presence of streetlamps and house lights is something of an annoyance after the peaceful darkness of the journey here.

My home town is situated in such a way as to be located between the surf beaches of the Gower peninsula so loved by Clive Gammon, and the rough ground of Ogmore Deeps, Witches Point and beyond meaning that sometimes, when I set the scale sliding to decide where to fish, I can often fall on a shadier middle ground somewhere between the two, where surf beach conditions give way to a rockhopper's paradise. In terms of fishing, this can often throw up a few unexpected surprises.

*

At last, here is a sky to do justice to Elle's painted pebbles: gin-clear, and filled to the brim with stars, so much so that I don't know what to do with them all. Aside from a handful of the better-known constellations like ursa major and draco remembered from a passing boyhood fascination, they simply look like an endless shimmering expanse of moon-silver desert sands to me; enough, apparently, to outnumber the Earth's actual grains of sand ten times over though thinking about such amounts begins to boggle me.

Still looking up, I lift the box from the car, showering grains of sand everywhere – into the air, down my neck, in my eyes. Perhaps there are more grains than those scientists thought after all. Over the years, I could swear I've gradually shifted an entire beach in the boot of the car. After I'm long dead, they'll discover somewhere beneath my garden a seam of sand laid down as a deposit over the decades.

Interesting as all this may be, I'm not so much bothered about the numbers than the fact that I'm finally able to look up and marvel on such clarity, one of the plus points of fishing a very dark beach with the low levels of light pollution.

How things will pan out tonight I don't know. Perhaps my leanings toward shadow will pay off and I'll manage to pull a fish or two from the water, lay them upon the beach like a wet footprint left glistening where some selkie stole up the beach and disappeared into the darkness.

And if they don't? Well, never mind; there's always, the return along those country lanes, the odd badger, fox or bat flitting through the beams, and the light of Saint Mary Magdalene to guide me on my journey home.

IV – Year's Turning

Waiting for a Hunter's Moon

'...the secret ministry of frost
Shall hang them up in silent icicles,
Quietly shining to the quiet Moon.'

- *from 'Frost at Midnight' by Samuel Taylor Coleridge*

I have a fascination with death.

Before I go on, perhaps I should qualify this statement a little. I am no Jack-the Ripper in waiting, nor do I harbour any clandestine Pharaonic ambitions to be embalmed in readiness for the afterlife. Although, thinking about it, perhaps I should make arrangements for my rods and reels to accompany me to the grave. I couldn't bear the thought of anyone else getting their hands on them when I finally shuffle off my wellies for the last time. No, the deaths to which I refer, and with which I've had an abiding fascination for as long as I can remember, are those of the seasons.

The reason I mention this is because I'm witnessing one right now, ambling along the renovated tarmac footpath of my local river toward the estuary. As I write, it is late summer, eight thirty in the evening, and it is glorious, but I know that none of this can last. I know this because, paradoxically, at the moment, the air around me is literally alive – clouds of gnats and other small insects are blooming into the air, setting off the chains of life that hang sequentially from them: birds darting in and out of the scene and even a few bats, out early, flickering in and out of my peripheral vision like the shadow of something half-remembered.

Even the river has started to forget, its slow, pondering course sliding under the trees, past the rocks until the glassy surface is shattered by the sudden rising of a trout slashing at the surface like a sudden epiphany then disappearing again, its exquisite self-tailoring smoothing out its own ripples before the meditative route continues further downstream where the mullet hold sway over the tidal section that meanders finally down to the sea.

Before this footpath and the new section of road had been built further along, this whole area was wonderfully neglected – old factories and portakabins that would once have been filled with overall-clad men, closed up for one final time and abandoned to their own ruin and the adventures of young boys.

The Derelicts

Like that corner of the ancient maps
that said *Here be Dragons,*
they sat at the edge of our known world,
a lonely corner of a concrete sea.

A place to test your courage by.

Juddering sheet-steel skin
flayed down to ribs
shrieking across the wind
brought us running
to be swallowed whole,
toe-to-heel across the rotting planks,
bricks thudding into a murk
thick with the must of days
totted on calendars peddling oil and tyres.

Some of us would scramble on
alone to reach the furthest dark corners
emerging later with a grand manner,
a faraway look that swatted away
question after question on the walk home
when we left the derelicts to sink
back into their own extinction.

Of course, the fact that this area was largely ignored or, at most, simply passed through on a journey to somewhere else, made it a perfect area for wildlife to flourish all but unhindered. Often, coming back from our escapades around the lake, we were able to crouch unseen in the rushes and watch the occasional fox and, more often, a small colony of rabbits that inhabited the local scrubland. A couple of times a week over an entire summer we would watch them lollop about, imagining ourselves as hunters planning how best to bring down our prey. Should we play the waiting game and set a trap, perhaps? Or should we take the more proactive route, lurking with our pockets full of river pebbles, to emerge suddenly, slingshots whirring in the air above our heads? When we did eventually emerge from our hiding place, they'd instantly vanish into thin air, dispersing like a handful of blown sand.

Then one day, near summer's end, we ambled up as usual, crouched into position and saw…nothing. Not a trace of a rabbit or anything else. We strolled over to the open area to investigate and almost tripped over something that looked like a discarded sweater in the grass. Only when we looked more closely could we make out a pair of ears sticking out from beneath, then the feet, tossed to one side, and finally the small, neat pile of viscera glistening wetly nearby. "Gypsies," my father suggested, "or maybe air rifle hunters. Either way, they're getting rid of a pest. There's thousands of the buggers in that dockland." You could have fooled us though, as never again did we see another rabbit in that area.

People are often surprised when I tell them this story, as though places such as this should only exist as they do in landscape watercolours, forever picturesque and untainted by the negative. The truth is that this river and its outlying areas, like all others, sees quite a lot of death in many different ways, my most recent experience of it coming only a week or so ago, a little further along the same path I'm strolling now.

I was startled to see so many people. Normally the weir section of the river is a passing place, a conduit for joggers, dog walkers and beachcombers homing in on a tide retreating down the beach a few hundred yards ahead. A quiet, unremarkable section of water, the only noise usually comes from an occasional "Hello" as I pass one of those people mentioned, or the slop of a wind-chop on the river slapping wavelets up the hulls of the scant collection of bobbing fishing boats moored there, but there was a strange, low hum of chatter coming from a small knot of people that had coagulated around the weir pool at half-tide.

Amongst them was Phil, a friend, who nodded a cursory "Alright mate?" as I ambled up.

"What's going on, Phil?"

"See for yourself, mate", he nodded down toward the pool. It had been filled to the level of the weir by the incoming tide but hadn't yet spilled over push on upstream to the level above it.

I watched for a moment, trying to discern something, anything, in the river's murky soup, before my attention was caught by a dull pewter flash, then another and another, like some erratic monochromatic semaphore, as the arrowhead shape of a sewin twisted and turned and hustled around the pool. At first, I struggled to see what had agitated the fish, until its next flashing turn was quickly covered by the glide of a fleeting, dark shadow.

Only two days before I had been startled by this same shadow while perched on a rock next to a mirror-calm sea. As I focused on my line dandling between the rocks in the tide, a large black head rose slowly like a dark moon only a few feet from where I was sitting and, in the low light, it took a little squinting before I made out the whiskers and huge eyes watching me intently from where the seal bobbed placidly as it took a break from its breakfast hunt.

And now here it was again, flickering in and out of solidity as it fell into a strangely beautiful but obscene dance with the sea trout it was chasing, looping outward then arcing back time and again so that, to those of us privileged enough to be watching, it seemed they might spend eternity locked like that. Out and back, out and back, then, at last, it was done.

The water flared, then dulled.

The tide pushed on.

A lot of the onlookers, particularly those unaccustomed to seeing such things, muttered words like "sad" and "shame", in that way that someone might tut at television images of a pride of lions eating an antelope. *Such is life…and death*, I felt like saying. *Lives end as days and seasons must end too*, but I caught the words in my throat, knowing that they would probably sound trite, so I left it alone, thinking it ironic that these people could be so moved by this one death, the most natural thing in the world, when all around them, the hugeness of the summer's expiration was beginning to play itself out.

Although Keats accepted the coming of autumn as something of a sombre occasion, heard when "the small gnats mourn", I find it difficult to see anything as being less than positive amongst all this change and decay. When it comes to Romantic poetry, my sympathies have always fallen more with Wordsworth's "…sweet mood when pleasant thoughts/Bring sad thoughts to the mind," his recognition that there must always be this balance, that without the bad against which to measure it, we can never fully appreciate what is good. If the old adage *It's always darkest before the dawn* has truth to it, then so must the inverse: before the darkness there must be a final spectacular flare of life and colour, as though the world had considered the options and had finally come to be at peace with the change that it knew must come.

Sometimes, that change is more rapid in coming than others. I'll know it when it does happen, following the lapsang souchong aroma through the house to the back door, to be greeted with a much stronger smoky blast of air and a distant crackling sound. Around half a mile to the left of the house, a mountain fire will be sweeping the slopes of Mynydd Dinas, a low, creeping blaze that pares everything right back as it goes.

There's no danger of course; well, not to us at least, sitting on this side of the River Afan that separates us from the mountain (or hill to be more accurate, as it's some 150ft short of the 1000ft required of a true mountain) but for those few living across its slopes they must by now be used to the almost annual evacuation, the firemen stringing out across the slopes, doing their best to protect these properties and beat out the blaze.

It's often difficult to track these fires to their source: sometimes it is as simple as the wanton mindlessness of arson, at other times it may be a plastic bottle or a fragment of glass. Such small details, often overlooked, are always a reminder of that friction when habitation meets nature, a friction that can occasionally flare up beyond all control.

Walking the mountain's bare slopes after such a blaze is always an otherworldly experience akin, I imagine, to looking out upon a post-apocalyptic landscape: scorched earth, bare gradients and a blackened, charred sense of desolation hovering over everything.

Weirdly, though, for all this apparent negativity, there is always something positive to be taken from it. The clutter of bramble and fern, gorse and heather have been tidied away, opening up the view in all directions, and all those nutrients in the soil will ensure that through the next year, this mountain will sway with life in greens and yellow and purples once again.

This year there has been no fire, but all around a million little deaths have already begun. The mountain's slopes have been resplendent these last few months in its subtle summer plumage, but looking up this morning I noticed that the heather's purple hue, too fragile to last, has already begun to give up the fight and recede into a blanket of browns, leaving only the sparkling pin pricks of the gorse flowers to burn on and the fierce orange pyracantha berries on my way to work to hint at those streetlit mornings that are just around the corner. The bright bulbs of blackberries are bursting from their thickets as if in an early apology of abundance for the lean months to come; the trees are preparing for their abandonment by both the birds and the foliage that now screens them behind its defiant last blaze and even the sky has lost its impetus, sinking into an occluded palette of yellows, blues, reds and oranges that run together and bleed down toward the earth, mirroring the leaves and making it difficult to know where the trees end and the sky begins.

Without doubt this is a season nearing its end, and it is beautiful.

True, all I'm really looking at is a mass of countless refracting particles and an unpicked fretwork of light, but to bring science into the picture and think in such ways now would somehow sully this lovely evening. I defy anyone to stand and watch such a sunset as the one that I'm confronted with now and not feel at all moved. I have literally watched hundreds of these over the years, from dozens of different spots along the coast and hills around my home town, but this one stands out particularly, beautiful to such an extent that this riot of hues has focused me intensely for the time being, on colour.

Dylan Thomas once wrote the line

'Once, it was the colour of saying...'

a statement that at once blurs the boundaries between thought and speech, the real and imagined and all that they conjure up both on their own and together, but for my own purposes I would alter this to

'Once, it was the colour of angling'.

Every angler, whether they realise it or not, will at some point translate their fishing into colours, not to the point where it's glaringly obvious, or even perhaps realised at all, but to the point where it is ever present, a persistent indefinable *something* that creeps into the background every time they think of themselves with a fishing rod in hand, so that this particular colour will, in turn, draw in everything else like a magnet - sounds, smells, shadows and colours all cascading into the imagination in one collective sensory image.

Thus, for some, the deep, rich tones of racing green will forever catapult them immediately to an overgrown secluded pool, in turn firing off the smells of damp vegetation and rotting undergrowth; maybe the *purupup* of a moorhen begins to perforate the air and the skin begins to rise in goose pimples at the coolness of a deeply shaded swim barely accessible where it lies tucked between towering stands of reeds that part to reveal slivered glimpses of a huge carp silting the margins with a slow, dignified swish of its tail.

Or perhaps the colour is a mottled grey glimpsed momentarily in the drab surface of a supermarket car park, before immediately transforming into a scarified, rocky, cod-infested outcrop laced with the chill tang of salt spray, pierced by the skriking of gulls and thrumming to the deep THOOM of the tide smashing like a persistent siege engine into its base.

Even if you've only ever fished once in your life, the bright yellow of summer sunshine or the turquoise of the sea from which you pulled that thrashing mackerel will, inevitably and irrevocably, lodge somewhere deep in the brain so that some part of you will forever associate with that colour. For me, that colour is white.

In a few weeks from now, we will have weathered the worst of the early equinoctial storms that are already beginning to sweep in, the clouds will be whisked aside like a magician's cape and suddenly, the sky will be pierced by a big pale gunshot that showers splinters of white everywhere. The Hunter's Moon will have arrived.

To many this is a time of depression, the darker months switching them into a kind of mental hibernation mode, but I differ. I've always been one of those who prefer dusk to dawn, autumn to spring. Perhaps, as I'm relatively young and, hopefully, have a few decades to spare yet, I am allowing myself this indulgence while I can. Revisit me when I've another twenty years under my belt and perhaps the reverse will be true.

For now, though, the autumn/winter season is a time of quiet indulgence, when the world holds its breath in anticipation and stops to think. Everything begins to empty – the trees of their leaves, the skies of their birds and the streets of people, and the world is effectively zeroed so that whichever way you turn you are confronted with a hundred thousand cold, gilded edges and one huge empty clean slate.

For centuries, human beings across the world have prepared and waited for this point in the calendar. All those other sdpartan, portioned-out waxy impostors in the skies of previous months were forgotten, and for all manner of indigenous peoples from Native Americans to Europeans of all derivations, the period between the Harvest moon of September and October's Hunter's moon arrived to mark its significant point in the year, a major temporal staging point in life's journey. Traditionally, this would be a time when harvests were gathered in and livestock slaughtered in readiness for the coming months of hardship. Whole villages would gather en masse in the fields and drills, the children taken out of school to gather in the harvest, working through long days and on into the nights, the light from the big full moons and the relative lack of darkness between sunset and moonrise allowing for longer working hours, the process being best described by Longfellow in his poem *The Harvest Moon*:

> It is the Harvest Moon! On gilded vanes
> And roofs of villages, on woodland crests
> And their aerial neighbourhoods of nests
>
> Deserted, on the curtained window-panes
> Of rooms where children sleep, on country lanes
> And harvest-fields, its mystic splendour rests!
>
> Gone are the birds that were our summer guests,
> With the last sheaves return the labouring wains!
> All things are symbols: the external shows
>
> Of Nature have their image in the mind,
> As flowers and fruits and falling of the leaves;
> The song-birds leave us at the summer's close,
> Only the empty nests are left behind,
> And pipings of the quail among the sheaves.

Living in a time of convenience and plenty, the importance of harvest time doesn't quite hold the same life-or-death significance for me as it did for many in Longfellow's day. The only Kilner jar in my house is the one upon the desk in my study, that brims over with an odd assortment of pens rather than some variety of hedgerow preserve, yet somehow, despite the disappearance of Harvest Home, the season's "mystic splendour" endures, the endlessly repeating symbolism still remaining as significant to me as it did to my forebears, and so I prepare carefully, as did all generations before me, to pass through the gateway to winter.

Whereas their preparations would certainly have included butchering stock, salting and smoking meat, gathering in crops and grain and the cutting and storing up stocks of firewood, mine are all of an angling nature.

First come the rods and reels. Rod rings are checked over for chipped liners that would shear line in an instant, and their whipping given a thin coat of high build to cover those exuberant hairline cracks of a summer smooth hound session; reels are stripped down, washed, oiled, tuned and loaded with new line, checking the balance of the spools for smoothness of casting, all important when hurling a bait into the relentless headwinds.

Next the rigs: new rigs are tied – the tried and trusted and maybe a few experimental patterns to top up the rig wallets; hooks are renewed, snoods re-tied wherever necessary.

The petrol lamp is stripped down and serviced, mantles replaced, and the tetra can of petrol that will help to run it through those long cold nights is topped up to brimming.

Finally comes the bait. First, I'll drive a few miles along the coast to dig a few pounds of lugworms ready to be salted and bagged up in twenties as a back-up or to bulk out large fresh worm bait for the cod shoals, then maybe I'll sneak in a last session on the mackerel if the weather is calm or, as now, I'll head down to the estuary to gather mussels, razorfish, and maybe scrape out a few sandeels or straggling peeler crabs if it's been warm enough. When these are done, when "all is safely gathered in/ere the winter storms begin", then I'll know I'm ready for the winter season.

*

The weeks move on.

Everything sharpens, becomes more focused; a time of clarity and infinitesimal detail in which I'll sit waiting for a bite and watching the particles of frost feathering out in intricate patterns across the grey canvas of my rod holdall as the bait does its best to re freeze.

From Friday through to Sunday, and occasional evenings in between, looking up through the cloud of steam over the rim of a Thermos cup will offer a view across beaches garlanded with little islands of icy white light thrown out by LED headlamps, and by the warm saffron coloured nimbus of the occasional petrol lantern, pinpointing each angler strung out along the bay like little stations of warmth on a journey away into the dark nowhere. The air becomes so clear and sharp that across the channel the lights of Devon and Somerset twinkle hopefully against the blackness. What do they look like? How quiet are their streets, those little villages and towns tucked in against the cold? Are there any anglers out there on beaches facing me, staring back through clouds of their own breath, wondering about the distant lights of Wales?

Even though language fails across such freezing miles, even though there can be no communication at this distance, those distant, imagined faces and I are linked by what surges alive between us. Beneath the water's dark calm, millions upon millions of whiting, pouting, dab and, of course, codling will have begun their annual invasion of our inshore waters so that everyone who ventures out to wet a line at this time of year is united by a common purpose. All around this sweep of coastline anglers of Wales and the West country alike are plugged into what flows through the currents of autumn and sustains us through to February, so very far away on the other side of winter's icy grip.

But all of this is still weeks away, weeks that seem like a lifetime as I watch the sun finally burn down into its own grave behind Swansea to the west.

Still, I've waited this long for the Hunter's Moon, and those weeks will pass quickly enough, as they have through every seasonal cycle stretching back through time, and as they surely must again.

From here on, the autumn will arrive and then pass in stages. Back on the treadmill of work and day-to-day life I'll barely have time to notice the changes come, stopping only here and there to notice that the trees have altered in appearance or that, suddenly, there seems much less daylight than the previous week, and so the year will have almost slipped by me before I'm wise to it.

I've always promised myself that one year, when I finally win the lottery, or when some unknown, distant relative leaves me a million in their will, I will exchange one year of my life for twelve months in Japan. There, I would follow Basho's trail to the deep north upon which, in exchange for that year and a few "frosty hairs on my head", I shall take a full twelve months' worth of seasons, wandering through the spring's cherry blossom, maybe look for higher altitudes to avoid the humidity of early summer's rainy season. But most of all, I will allow myself to take back the period from late August through to the year's conclusion.

I will wait patiently for the calendar to slip on through September. I will wait for the coloured season to make its slow progress from the north, advancing in a slow-motion wave from Hokkaido, then southward through Honshu, Shikoku and Kyushu.

I will wait for this wave to break, following it south and taking part in Momijigari, or *searching for the red leaves*, visiting the most beautiful places where I will stroll down avenues of orange, yellow, red and gold, some of them lit for maximum effect, where, like many Japanese people, I will enjoy being an emperor of such small pleasures. Perhaps one day.

Until then, I will have to content myself with these snatched glimpses taken from my classroom window, my seatbox upon a beach, or a river path like this one where, in the trees beside me, the first leaves give up and tumble back and forth, from side to side in their erratic pantomime, swaying from side to side as though there were another place to land, some other way to fall.

Last Look

A scream burst the silence last night, echoing from tile to mirror, wall to door and on through the ground floor of the house, probing with a needle point shrillness that pierced the heart and the gut. My daughter shrieked again: "Daddy! Daddy! Come quickly!"

Sprinting to bathroom, my mind was racing; what was wrong? Strange noises outside, perhaps? A pale face peering in at the window? I burst through the door to be confronted with my daughter's terrified face and…a house spider. Admittedly, it was a leggy beast, but it didn't put up much of a challenge as I picked it up and popped it out through the back door.

"Weather's turning," the old wives would say; "they're looking for somewhere warm to sleep." I don't think it's sleeping that's on their minds, but I think there's some truth that the weather's about to take a turn, though it doesn't look that way at the moment.

The day began unexpectedly early, the dawn chorus barging its way through the open bedroom window. First, a stonechat kik-kik-kick started proceedings, rapping out its desire to enter my morning. Its short shift done, it then moved over for a wren to take its turn, doing its best to soothe the situation, its song somewhat more pleasant to the ear.

Time to get up. If the weather was good enough to get the birds so enthusiastic, it was high time I stepped out and took a look for myself.

When I did finally look outside it was indeed glorious, but it felt somewhat like I'd stepped back in time. Everything had been mottled in the colours of a Victorian country parsonage, complete with the displays of flora and fauna that proliferate in every niche. Plants hung heavy under the cobwebby stillness of the day like dusty old damask curtains in a forgotten bedroom, and everywhere there were varying shades of vermilion, deep green, coppery burnt orange and teak browns.

I stepped out into the garden to get a closer look and, turning back round to grab my coffee, there they were: three orb weavers, much more brazen than their housebound cousins, exactly where they had unpacked themselves like tinkers in the night, attaching their anchor lines to the guttering just above the back door. Shiny as brass tacks, they seemed to hover casually at eye level, coronal at the centre of their respective webs, surrounded by constellations of struggling midges.

Two had anchored the other end of their webs between the shed and the holly bush in the corner, splaying across the planted border in a gossamer V, twin watchmen for whatever might fly past.

Two steps to the right brought about a beautiful change of perspective as the three webs slowly lined up almost perfectly behind one another, the same fractal image thrown across different sections of a broken mirror. Quite an apt image really, as it's very much a time of reflection now.

I had thought that the summer had already died. September arrived and brought with it low pressure systems, bands of rain and a drop in temperatures. Returning to work after the summer holidays, within the first few days I had already christened my new winter jacket.

But here we are, October and…

Tsss! The cider bottle opens with an admonishing tut, as though to tell me that such indulgence at eight in the morning is plainly not a good idea. Not to worry. I slide the open bottle along the kitchen worktop with the other ingredients: four ounces of plain flour; two of wholemeal; baking powder; sugar; butter; eggs and apples.

The irony is not lost on me – cooking a Harvest cake with ingredients I've bought in a supermarket. Living within a hundred and fifty yards of the front door of one of the "big four" supermarkets makes for lazy shopping habits and a life of convenience. In fact, for the most part, there's not much opportunity around here to actually harvest any such ingredients. Aside from a few blackberries and cherries, we are forced to rely on the shops for everything these days. Still, we must make the best of it. Everything is mixed together, poured into the tin and, in just over an hour, supermarket ingredients or not, there will be a Harvest cake plated up and ready to eat.

Harvest is one of my favourite times of year. Just the mention of the word conjures to mind distant memories of carrier bags filled with tins and packets that would be piled up in the school hall. Daily we would watch the stack grow as we spent our days drawing wheat sheaves and writing poems about crops and weather before gathering in the hall to belt out hymns like 'We plough the fields and scatter' and delivering hampers of our collected goodies to various elderly folks in the area.

Although this doesn't seem to be as prevalent in our schools of late, some residual awareness of these agricultural seasons lives on in less rural areas. I for one am grateful that my interest in sea angling has given me both knowledge and awareness of the changing seasons, something that I later also found deeply rooted within the liturgical year. And so there will just be time for me to take the cake from the oven to cool, and to clean up before going off to the Benefice Harvest Mass.

The organ's already playing as I approach the doors, and almost unavoidably, I am struck with the reversal of this whole process. I think of those peasant labourers and yeoman farmers who would have brought the fields and the crops, the bread and the wheat sheaf into their country churches to fill the aisles with the relief and plenty of the Harvest season. Now, of course, the reverse is true. The sense of bounty is all in relation to how full the shop shelves are; all the necessity of prayer and anxiousness far removed from this time of year for most people. Yet still the churches open their doors and pour out their music and prayer, offering something back to the modern world from the storehouses of worship they have stocked over the centuries. The Mass begins with 'Come Ye Thankful People, Come', an old favourite from my school assembly days, immediately cocooning me in that strange sense of the half-familiar that is at once comforting and yet somehow renews the original memory as it taps into the past, both distant and more recent.

Father Rhun begins his sermon, relating the story of a

fisherman encouraged to expand his fleet and become more business-like so that he can expand further still and so, eventually, retire in luxury. I recognise it as a reworking of section 22 of Traherne's first *Century* in which Pyrrhus, the King of Epire intends to go out and conquer half the world so that he may return home triumphant, to spend his days enjoying himself at home. In Father Rhun's story, the fisherman turns the questions upon his interrogator: "Why should I go out and do that?"

"Why", replies the man, "so that you can retire and sit here, relaxing and enjoying yourself".

"And what do you think I'm doing now?" responds the fisherman.

It is a good story, and well chosen, both for the time of year and for the age in which we live. I agree that our society seems never to be satisfied without having the latest thing, the newest, fastest, shiniest, most expensive gadget. John Clare, one of the writers I most associate with this time of year, would have agreed too; his hatred of the ways in which modernisation and progress changed tradition, sentiment and the countryside he so loved looming large in mood and word throughout his days.

The Mass ends and we walk out into the early autumn sunshine. St. Luke has clambered his way back from the gospels to give us the rather Bacchanalian excess of his little summer, transforming everything into a living paragraph that could have been lifted from the pages of Adrian Bell or Laurie Lee. It's a beautiful day and I have lots of time to spare: Time perhaps for tea and a slice of that cake and then, I think, time enough for a few hours of fishing.

*

I'd said I would pack up ten minutes ago. While I've got the afternoon free, I really should clean out the gear after a long and indulgent summer season, but though some days lumber on through their hours and others just stop like an old clock, a handful, like this one, as though just to prove time's relative elasticity, stretch on for a bit longer. If my encounter with those spiders this morning meant anything, and if this really is a time of reflection, of looking in nature's mirror, then like some teenager back and forth in two minds in front of that mirror, I must put up with a fair degree of indecisiveness in this month that's retrospective and forward-facing at the same time. This is echoed in my choice of tackle or, rather, my lack of choice, for I seem to have tipped out the shed and brought all of it.

Today I have tried legering, spinning, feathering and float fishing, all of which have offered up various results. Nothing much to the spinning or feathering rods but it was fun to watch the float slide gently away a few times due to the attentions of small pollack and school bass. Now I'm at last knockings, or perhaps last-but-one knockings, having reduced everything down to just one bottom-fished rod. All day it's been picking up random scraps – a random flounder here, an eel there and, an hour ago, a beautiful red gurnard that came flaming out of the water. Now it's rapping again. Nothing big, but its insistence continues. Seeing as bringing it in would mean the end of the session I'll leave it out a little longer. There's always a little time yet – there it goes again – to soak up a little more, kind of like a swimmer taking a big breath before going under again.

I know this spot very well. In fact, as I'm sitting here, I can see a hundred other sessions happening, most of them busier than this one, all of them involving daydreams and thoughts of some kind, the fortunate by-products of angling that led Izaak Walton to refer to it as 'The Contemplative Man's Recreation'. And so, naturally, I begin to think about thinking, about all those things I pondered my way through during those sessions, from exams and girlfriends and, above all else, those many hours spent looking forward to things – being older, first beer, learning to drive, a job (and money for fishing tackle) of my own, leaving home, as though everything good were yet to come, an attitude that transferred to my fishing days. I fished hard and greedily through consecutive tides, foregoing the formality of sleep, as though it would get in the way of the next fish. Everything was about the now and about what was yet to come and, more importantly, about getting hold of it there and then.

I could never understand how the grown-ups in my life, particularly my grandparents and great aunts and uncles, were constantly looking back and reminiscing as though all the good things had already happened and should be cherished before the memory of them faded too much. Did they not realise that the past was gone, that here and now was where it was all happening? But such impatience is for the very young. Although no veteran, I have reached a stage of life in which I'm quite happy, slung between the past and the future like a hammock, letting time and action and memory roll and accumulate around me, dropping in from all sides.

Usually, one of my angling sessions is an organised thing. It has to be – baits, species and tides need to coincide in order to provide a relative degree of success, but here, now, there's no need for such organisation. Sometimes we all need a cobbled-together rag-bag of a day, a proverbial loosening of the belt. Today is mine, as evidenced in the random assortment of objects scattered around me – radio, flask, sandwiches. There's even a book for the quiet stretches and, of course, a notebook for all those thoughts about thoughts. I think that even the fisherman in Father Rhun's story would approve of this.

A little turnstone that has been puttering around, picking little bits of bait here and there, has come back to me. He seems happy enough, like a little kid scooching in and out of the rocks, making me think of Adrian Bell's assertion that "adult life is no more than a mock-up of the serious business of childhood". A good assertion it is too, prompting me into action. With this in mind, I decide that there's just enough time left for something a little different, or maybe that should read *time for something completely original* – the most original, in fact.

Ignoring the superfluous rods and reels and unwinding twenty or so feet of line from a spare spool, I attach a size 8 hook and a couple of shot to the end of the line. Now I'm like that stonechat from this morning, kick-kicking at a limpet, struggling to loosen it just as much as I did the first time I ever did this. Finally, a sliver of limpet meat is added to the hook and the whole lot is lowered down the side between the rocks. It doesn't take long. Fishing like this, with a simple line running through my hands is not a million miles away from how my grandfathers would have fished here fifty years ago. Back then, when the wooden upper tier of this breakwater was intact, the town's young men used to come down here with simple hand lines made of heavy Dacron attached to a simple brass-boomed double paternoster end rig that was swung out over the sides in search of cod. Ironic, really, that I'm sitting here surrounded by hundreds of pounds' worth of carbon rods and reels with their engineered gears and yet I find myself tethered to old fashioned memory. In quick succession a flurry of two shore crabs and four gobies scratch the itch and flip me back into the present, back to that rattling rod that can no longer be ignored.

Maybe this is why this session is just so laid back and, well, poised between past and present. Maybe I'm not just haphazardly slung into some metaphorical hammock watching the hours pass but am balanced perfectly at that midpoint where I have as many fishing sessions left in my life as I have already used up. Maybe I'm just talking rubbish, and I have only a few dozen sessions left, or perhaps I'm lucky and have many hundreds. Time can be like this sometimes; or rather, the way we see time can be like this, so perhaps it's better not to put too much faith in anything but the now, even if it is very fleeting. By the time you come to read this, the moment will no longer be time present but will have slipped into time long past, existing only upon this page and in my memory.

But for the time being I can assure you that I am most definitely present, enjoying the last dregs of this afternoon where I am perched on one of the rocks so that my rod reaches out over the snags in the quickly-retreating tide and the reel's handle can rotate its steady rhythm unhindered, bringing in to me the culprit responsible for those rattles.

A gentle chill has just begun to slide in off the back of the sea as I reel in…ah, no great surprise - a tiny little whiting, the first at this back half of the year. In my palm its ragged little white outline looks just like a torn-off piece of envelope, or a hastily handwritten note perhaps, scribbled down and passed on as a reminder that winter won't be long now.

Genus: Piscator

A quiet afternoon in the garden, perhaps the last for this year.

I topped up our wine glasses, then sat back again to enjoy the advancing evening as the day started to wind down. The traffic out on the streets was blurring to a gentle haze of noise and even the M4 link that bisects the town was reduced to whispers, as though snatches of murmured conversation were falling from the windows of the cars as they passed.

The immediate landscape (if that can ever be the correct choice of word to describe a town centre street) around the garden is a clutter to the eye. Above the level of the wall the skyline is dominated by washing line posts, telegraph poles and street lights, all stacked up in close urban proximity like a fleet of concrete and creosote masts becalmed in the still evening.

Then, BAAA! A burst of sound as close as though the sheep were only twenty yards away, and suddenly I was focusing beyond the posts and poles, my eyes working like one of those soft cinematic dolly zooms that melted the foreground away until they came to rest upon the top of Mynydd Emroch a couple of miles away from where I stood. The low sun was striking the flank of the hill, casting it in a pink glow where a small flock of sheep grazed the slope.

How little we really see things, I thought to myself, until a small change allows some new reality to make itself known, opening up other angles and vantage points from which to look at the world around us, in this case a drop and swift shift in the prevailing winds that carried the bleating of some distant sheep right up to my garden wall.

We both felt the change in the wind, shift slightly in our seats and so, autumn breezed in, not too fast, trailing a hint of coolness like fresh news.

Though neither of us mentioned it yet, we both knew that this subtle change had just occurred. Not enough to make anyone stop or lurch in surprise, but enough to make us feel that new directions were being taken, in the way that someone senses the progression of a journey whilst slumped half-asleep in the passenger seat of a car.

The end of October was nearing. For the previous few weeks, I looked on as the world around me buzzed and crackled with life like a van der Graaf generator so that everywhere I turned, it seemed that life was going into overdrive.

Throughout the summer I was lucky to spot as little as a handful of squirrels each time I went out - their skittish rustlings always seemed to be two steps ahead of me wherever I went; but only a fortnight previously my daughter and I, out for a walk in a local country park, lost count of the number we saw bolting through the undergrowth. Everywhere we turned, we seem to stumble across half buried acorns.

Lately, they seemed to be far less aware of us, so much so that we were able to get within five feet of them on occasion. In fact, now I think about it, this is true of most of the local woodland critters as they all scamper around gathering, nesting and collecting, and why shouldn't they?

The fragile and finely balanced little ecosystems that bring our countryside to life through the spring and summer face down the barrel of yet another cold, hard winter and as though on autopilot, they have furiously locked into their annual survival routine, laying down what little they can before the first hard frosts begin to bite.

In their scurrying around, they reminded me of little firefighters trying their futile best to damp the world back down as it erupted around them, leaf by leaf, into a billion new flames. Soon they will lose their battle; both the trees and the woodland's floor will be ablaze.

A few days after the squirrel-spotting session my daughter came barrelling into the house, her friend in tow, shouting "Daddy! Daddy! Come quick; you've got to see this!" A small hedgehog snuffled through the gutter at the end of our street. It couldn't stay here where it would undoubtedly end up as roadkill on the town centre tarmac, but carefully picking it up and placing it in an old washing up bowl ready to take to the local riverside woodland, I could feel just how light and thin it was and realised that it would have to stay up late looking for food or it wouldn't survive the winter.

We gave it a plate of cat food and then took it to be released and, as I watched it sniff and stumble off through the long grass in search of its next meal, I began to think that in many respects, we humans are not much different. Watch the footage of some humanitarian tragedy on the evening news and you'll see the similarities in behaviour - masses of human beings blindly stumbling around, guided and driven only by the body's sheer will to keep going, muscle memory and, to a much greater extent, sheer instinct, filling in the void left by the absence of logical, conscious thought. The human race often likes to congratulate itself on how wonderfully intelligent it is, but when the programming goes wrong, instinct is always there as a saving grace, the last line between us and extinction.

The light started to fail, so we decided to have five more minutes before collecting everything up and heading indoors.

Equinoctial

Across my lap this broken paperback
Waits for the moon's half-truth
To cast its story in a different light.

A hill breeze we can't hear
Teases a mime routine from the firs:
Such eloquence in the silence of trees.

Wind chimes percolate
Their rumour through the garden,
Each ring the trill of coming rain.

Unlike you, I lack control
Of that instinct that tells you when
To sleep, to breathe, to turn for home;

The one that sees you so exact
As to arrive at our front door
At the first touch of drizzle,

That has you now casting your eyes
Upwards at the gathering cloud
Filling these hollowed skies,

And clutching the shawl closer to
Your throat, your breast,
As though gathering windfalls.

By the time that we finally finished the wine and began to head inside, the feeling that autumn had most definitely arrived was becoming harder and harder to shake, though it wasn't an entirely unpleasant thought, knowing what the season brings.

Ever since I was a young boy I've loved this season above all others even down to its name drawing a satisfactory, appreciative hum from the mouth, and when you come to love something you take possession of it, harbour a desire to defend it against all-comers, especially foreign pretenders to the title such as the American *Fall*. I hated that idea as a kid, the fact that such a lovely time of year could be named after a simple mishap. Every time I tried out the imposter it just felt wrong on the lips, creating mental images of grazed knees and scuffed toecaps. It was only after having studied some of that country's greatest writers at university, luminaries such as Thoreau, Emerson, Longfellow, Whitman and Frost, that I finally came to appreciate the Fall.

Theirs seemed a fresher, newer look at the world born in a country founded upon endings and new beginnings, a full-blooded appreciation of what comes to be gained and lost and counted as it passes in a fledgling country as opposed to gentle lapping of the years at the foot of the great, unshakeable British Empire of the 19th century. A fleeting vision of what loss truly meant, as picked up here and there in the writings of retrospectively tragic figures such as Keats and Kilvert seemed to resonate even more and help me to see things differently, so that now, even though I love the autumn, I see how everything falls within it: the leaves fall, heads drop a little lower into coat collars; even the sky seems to be lowered like some great boom, bringing with it the rain.

Rain is so much a part of the British psyche that it can sometimes feel that the nation's bloodstream is diluted by rain water. We factor it into our plans, make allowances for it; at times it can feel like there's so much rain that it persists only to wash us all out of the way, our spirits and hearts sinking in a wet, grey barrage of newscasts about weather fronts and floods to come across the country.

And then, seemingly in response to my ramblings, the temperature, not to be outdone, also dropped slightly. It seemed to follow us coolly into the kitchen on our coat tails, chilling the air instantly, though, as always, it could never be said to be disagreeable, so we left the door and windows open for a few minutes to encourage it to spend a while indoors.

"What's up? You're miles away," Rachel said as she came in behind me.

"Oh nothing; just daydreaming. Nothing important." But it had already started. As Rachel continued to potter in a tinkle of glasses, I continued with these thoughts, coming to the realisation that, tragedy aside, by the same measure, we anglers are very much like those little woodland animals in our basic behaviour. When deciding where and when to wet a line the weather, wind, tides, moon phases and air pressure all have us sticking our proverbial noses into the air and sniffing away for all we're worth.

In fact, once a decision has been made and we arrive at our chosen venue, we actually become a very specific type of animal. Under all the breathable, waterproof clothing, the shelters and thermal boots, there lurks the apex predator, staring down a two hundred lumen beam from the top of the food chain to survey sandbars, gullies, rock features, tidal rips and overshadowed pools in order to gauge the best hunting ground for the night.

Although this idea may be a tad over the top, it is a little thought about fact that the only things separating anglers from, say, a lion or a bear are the abilities to articulate our predatory reasoning and to collate, assimilate and use data in our hunting. Essentially, we are all doing the same thing; it's just that some animals are a little more sophisticated in how they go about it. Swap the faint scent trail for fishy internet rumours, exchange the familiar rabbit runs or deer trails for a venue that is noted as productive in the diaries and you're not a million miles away.

I drew the curtains and switched on the lamp, the slight turn in the weather turning my mind over with it as I did so, sputtering every now and then like a lawnmower engine as it caught on the thought that it might, just might, be time for cod. And instantly, things began to gather momentum of their own accord.

I had a venue in mind, one that I hadn't fished before but had scoped out on a family day out during the summer, (see how the predatory mindset just takes over when given a chance?) noting it as a potential cod venue. A cursory glance at the online weather forecasts told me that the winds, westerlies pregnant with rain, would blow hard all week before dropping in speed and swinging to blow from the northwest on the evening that I was beginning to mentally pencil in, meaning that the sea at the venue would be left coloured and with a little movement, though it would have had the sting taken out of it by the switch in wind direction.

But what bait to take? Worms would be a must if I was to target cod, and in a heavy sea I would usually plump for the extra scent of lugworm, but the dying sea would perhaps call for me to opt for a compromise between scent and movement, taking instead half a pound of wriggling ragworms that would kick around and add enticing movement to the hook. As a supplement I would also take some sandeels and prawns, figuring that the stormy seas of the previous week would have torn through the sand leaving scores of dead and dying fish and shellfish in their wake.

The plan set, the bait chosen, I set off for my chosen spot to fish the last two hours of the ebb and the first of the flood. Driving to the beach was like being at the helm of a spaceship thanks to our having very recently changed the car – endless banks of lights and a slick dashboard that made my old car look like a rickshaw. Still, fuel economy was good, particularly useful if I wanted to fish further afield; and the boot was bigger, great to fit the box and bucket as well as my clothing, without having to make the back seat smelly.

I bumbled off down the road and had gone only twenty or so yards when I noticed a green arrow flash up in front of me. That was strange. A little further down the road and there it went again! It was only after a few hundred yards that I realised that the arrow was telling me when to change gear, not something I'd usually think about, or even have to think about. Really? Okay, that's new. Time for a bit of music.

NAME FUNCTION.

"Eh?"

NAME FUNCTION. PHONE, CD OR RADIO…

"Er, radio…please."

RADIO. FM OR MW?

"Um…FM."

NAME FREQUENCY

And on went my first ever full-blown conversation with a car.

Is this what we'd come to? Must I rely upon technology to help make my decisions? Where will we ever draw the line? I wondered, as I unpacked the car.

Suddenly, for no immediately apparent reason I recalled one night, years before, when I had fished a local breakwater. All through the evening and into darkness I fished the place as I had every other time, anchoring a baited rig hard on the sea bed. After a few biteless hours of standing around I had become too bored to watch the rod tip anymore and so rooted around in the tackle bag for something else, though at this point I wasn't quite sure what.

What was this at the bottom? My hand closed around something unfamiliar, and I pulled a green and clear plastic float from the bottom. Ah well, in for a penny… Even though I was fishing with a thirteen-foot beachcaster, something rather unsuitable for float fishing, I rigged up a float trace, lobbed the whole lot out a dozen yards and lay back on the rocks, staring up at the sky, and allowing myself to fall into a sleepy indolence.

After half an hour of aimless dreaming, the rod seemed to jump to life in my hands as something slammed into the bait. Lifting the rod and winding the reel through the darkness, I had no idea what was on the other end, or how the hell I was going to get it up the rocks, as the tide had ebbed to almost dead low.

With one final heave, I yanked the rig toward me and a bass of around two pounds appeared out of the darkness and slapped onto a rock three feet away from me. I was astonished. I had caught a fish, and it had all been done by feel. No sight or hearing had been involved at all.

Quickly, I rebaited the rig and cast back out. Over the next couple of hours, I pulled in a string of mackerel, all out of the dark, all on the float, all of them by feel alone.

A good memory, and one that reminded me that I needed no arrows to point me toward the waterline. I needed no conversation to find my way through the tackle box or the process of rigging up, and when I did cast, I would know that it had flown true and far enough, and would also know somehow, without question, that the fish wouldn't be too far away.

Keeping this memory at the front of my mind, I carried on toward the surf line, though I began to notice that with every step I took, I was gradually lifting, whilst walking, over a series of medium sized sandbars, then feeling the sharp bite of cold water droplets flicked over the tops of my wellies as I sploshed on through small gullies either side of them. Looking out to sea, it was clear from the breaking water and calmer patches behind, that this pattern was repeating itself out to sea for some distance.

The plan wasn't even thought about; it just sprang immediately to mind. Often the best things do – that insomniac walk that might see you catching a family of foxes at their dawn hunting just before heading home for sleep or that final quick pint that is ordered just a minute before an old friend not seen for months happens to walk through the pub door.

One rod would be fished with a two-hook clipped up paternoster fished up to ninety yards. The hooks would be left flapping but could be clipped up for extra distance as and when needed. This would be fished on the inside edge of the sandbars facing me. On the second rod I clipped a two hook Portsmouth loop rig to deliver the baits a bit further out – up to one hundred and thirty yards, on the outer flanks of some of those small sandbanks. By fishing in this way, my bait would hopefully be trundling around in the natural food collection points.

Every so often, perhaps a handful of times a year, I'll turn up for a session and it will just feel…right. Conditions will appear to be perfect and I just know that I'll catch what I set out for. It can't be explained; it's just a feeling, but it's too strong to ignore and it's often right. In this session, I wanted to catch my first codling of the new autumn/winter season and, as the first bunch of ragworms was punched out to the far side of the sandbank, I felt that I would.

An hour later and I had virtually nothing to show for my efforts. From the very first cast, a combination of debris and a little tide consistently dragged my five-ounce breakout leads and baited rigs in huge, sweeping semi-circular arcs, garnishing the line with pounds of stringy weed. The forces that had so recently reshaped this beach were still in residence and clearly, they were not happy.

In response, I walked thirty yards up tide, casting even further in that direction so that the tide would eventually bring my lead roughly back to a position in front of where I stood, and this seemed to work, although I still only had two juvenile small-eyed rays to show for my efforts, lured by the addition of squid strip to my ragworm-baited double paternoster.

Still, I wasn't too worried yet. Anglers seem to be pre-programmed with this almost insane, "glass half full" kind of mentality; we always seem to think that better is to come. How many have used phrases like

'The fish will come on the feed when the light starts to fade'

or

'The best stage of the tide is yet to come'?

Animals in the wild will do this out of necessity – if some form of prey is not eventually caught, the cubs may well starve – but the fact that mod-cons have taken the necessity of the hunt away from modern mankind only means that anglers are left with a residual need to stay positive, to remain on the search, to spend that extra hour on the beach at four o clock on an October morning that is inexplicable. We call it optimism, others call it madness. My wife simply refers to it as *'bloody stupidity'*.

Even so, after a few hours, even my confidence was beginning to wane. I must have pulled over a hundred pounds of weed from the sea, used most of my bait and was still no closer to catching a codling. Still, the tide was about to turn, so the fish were bound to start feeding…

This was getting serious. Were my instincts going haywire? Then it came to me. Almost blinkered by my blind optimism, I hadn't paid much attention to the fact that the tide had changed. In a final, desperate throw of the dice, I immediately swapped rigs, exchanging the shorter snooded Portsmouth loop rig for an up and over – a bottom fished snood of over six feet long that clips onto the rig body in order to collapse it down for efficient casting. This would take advantage of the switch and increase in tidal movement, and the fact that the weed had eased slightly after the flood began. At the end of this a bunch of ragworms would waft and wave enticingly in the tide and surely tempt a hungry codling.

A bite! At least it looked a bit like a bite. It had only been fifteen minutes since the change and a single thud shimmered along the rod tip then died in the same movement. Abruptly, everything went slack, the rig sweeping off down tide after being broken out of the bottom, so that I was forced to snatch the rod from the stand.

Slowly, I cranked the rig back to shore by the steady rhythm – pump and wind, pump and wind. I was working hard for this fish, if indeed there was a fish on the end and not just more weed. This was almost insufferable; it seemed like it took an age to get the rig ashore! Finally, the leader knot pinged through the surf, somewhere under another twenty pounds of weed. Not now! The weed had gathered around the leader knot and jammed in the tip ring. Why does this always seem to happen at the worst time rather than on those fishless, quiet sessions? I was going to have to walk this one in, striding backwards, dragging weed and line as I went, all the while scanning the water's edge for the first sign of – a fish! There was definitely a fish there.

A plump two-pound codling, all freckles and rusted flanks, slid up the beach like a piece of storm-tossed flotsam, into my waiting hands, and there was no explanation needed, at least not in words, for this was justification in itself - the concept made flesh. Sometimes, no matter how expensive the rods and reels, how varied the bait and detailed the information, some fish will simply swim up and strike from somewhere far deeper than the shallow side of a sandbar.

Returning home later, I stowed the gear back in the shed and placed the cleaned fish in the fridge. Making a last cursory glancing check over everything before turning in, I lifted the paperback book I was reading earlier from the table just as the first drops of rain pattered across the glass tabletop.

This Sympathetic Magic

Quietly, and with a minimum of fuss, they have filed in and taken their places. It could be the fact that it's a Monday morning, or that it's cold and wet outside, but more than likely it's simply down to the time of year.

The murmuring susurration of voices dies away as the Assistant Head teacher steps up to take his place upon the stage in front of us all, his face tightened into a bead of concentration.

Everything is quiet aside from the sound of rain on the roof. In this hall building, the metal roof amplifies everything, so that the building storm outside sounds like a thousand windfalls.

When satisfied that all is in order he begins his recital and we, teachers and pupils alike, watch on in silence as the list of names reels up through the screen in time to his calling aloud and then

> *Eternal rest grant unto them, O Lord,*
> *And let perpetual light shine upon them,*

> *May they rest in peace,*
> *Amen.*

Pupils, staff, clergy; the names rise up across the screen like smoke, there one second and gone the next. Every year the list gets longer, takes slightly more time to read out, and all of us, child and adult alike, can't help but think that one day in the future somebody will be calling out our names, a fact made all the more real to those of us who remember the faces, the laughs, the tempers and the foibles of some of those names that now are nothing more than addenda to this collection of letters, something to which we will all eventually be reduced.

*

We file out of the doors as one mass under the weight of a

leaden sky. The rain is beginning to fall more heavily now, a rain that carries that sleety edge. The wind takes hold of the trees that line our left side, throttling leaves out of the branches and I'm reminded of an afternoon only a couple of days previous, and a falling of a different kind.

"What are they doing, Dad?" Elle asked as she, Rachel and I were strolling through a local park. "Come on, let's go and see." Forty yards or so ahead, a middle-aged couple had regressed to their childhood, leaping and giggling and scrabbling up at branches a few feet above their heads. Occasionally, they managed to catch hold of one, tugging at it repeatedly until it sent down a shower of conkers upon their heads, causing another burst of giggles and theatrical ducking before the whole thing started all over again.

No wonder it looked so alien to my daughter; conkering isn't something that is often seen these days, particularly in this neck of the woods, though in this case it did manage to conjure up the past and trigger some happy memories.

I reach my desk and sit awhile in the quiet classroom, the children all having gone to break, and continue to listen to the names still running through my head, one of them being Chris, a new addition to the list this year; a good man who had taken early retirement, and to whom I had chatted only a fortnight before his death, memories brought to mind hard on the heels of All Saints day and All Souls day, both having passed only a couple of days ago.

I come to, as if out of a trance, getting up from the desk to shake some life back into myself. The major plus point of my classroom is that it has half a wall full of windows that offer expansive open views. Looking down, I have an almost uninterrupted vantage point over the playground. *Thwack!* goes the football as it is hoofed from one end of the yard to the other. *Thwack!* Up it flies again, this time travelling farther and longer, through twenty-five years, landing now in my own primary school playground that resounds again to the thud of that football whacked back across its length every day. That is, until one day when one of the boys produced from his rucksack a bag of marbles.

Where he had got them from, I can't remember. Perhaps he'd found them in an old corner of his father's belongings, or maybe a grandparent had given them to him in a fit of nostalgia. Whatever was the reason, that first time he brought them in and emptied them rolling and glinting into my cupped hand like Burmese rubies and sapphires, kick-started a whole retro trend that ran throughout the school for weeks. The playground had fallen into a strange kind of twilit hush as dozens of groups of young heads closed in and hunched around the chalk circles that now peppered its concrete surface. Every day hopes were raised then dashed as prize marbles were won and lost and won back again, holding us all in suspense.

Until the arrival of conkers, that is.

"Have a look at this, boys" Dave had said, producing from his bag a handful of conkers suspended from some manky old shoe laces that looked as though they had been dredged up from the inside of a bin. "My dad was showing me how to play last night." Sceptical, three of us took up a conker and followed his instructions until, within five minutes, those conkers became our world. All other things were quickly twisted out into a fuzzy haze of inconsequential background as our whole world, no, our whole existence – life, future, death – hung dependant on our obliteration of the other boys' conkers. Nothing else mattered.

After our first taste we spent weeks traipsing through the overgrown lakeside and docklands looking for chestnut trees and then, afterwards, nagging our elders for information that saw us drying, pickling and baking and all sorts of various combinations of the three. Then, it was back to the yard every day, every fibre of my being centred on the conker that was hanging there from the string in front of me, and on smacking it as hard as I could.

Like all phases, conkers soon passed on. Not long after I would begin the longest of them all, a phase that came to overshadow all the others.

Just as antiquated in its way, garnered from the same source, fishing was the original old-fashioned hobby. Strangely enough, although I remember exactly who started the marble and conker crazes, and when they happened, I forget exactly when the fishing craze first broke out amongst us. As it didn't matter then, so it doesn't matter now. All that does matter is that we somehow contrived to turn up at lakesides, beaches, riverbanks and breakwaters with dusty, antiquated tackle. Like conkers, many of us took it up at an early age and embraced it wholeheartedly until it consumed us body and soul, but I watched on as the years passed and, one by one, team sport, girls, work, drinking and even drugs chipped away at that number until all the others had fallen by the wayside, leaving me as the last angler of my year group, feeling older than my years and more than happy to be so.

*

Looking up from the yard, I am afforded the even more impressive advantage of having a classroom overlooking the nearby hills. A huge, gently curving barometer for the seasons, I spend my break times and lunch breaks wishing away the days between holidays, watching on as the sunlit flanks turn green then red and brown, are gently disrobed or scantily covered in the finest veil of mist before turning green again. They are my lodestar to the passage of time here, particularly in these months of the year. By them I chart the seasons of new pupils, the departure of those now grown up, colleagues who have retired and, more recently, the accumulating years of my own career.

In this premature dusk their persistent presence reaches back through this day, week, year, century, and keeps on digging back until it reaches a time before the organised remembrance of names in a centrally heated, insulated assembly hall.

Centuries ago, around this time of year, hilltops like these would have been alive and dancing with fire, the great bonfires of Samhain, the Celtic festival to celebrate the close of Harvest season and to steel the local population for the dark months ahead, their dancing frivolity flickering in front of the growing flames whilst all around them air trembled and the trees dropped shadows to the ground, sending them shambling around like puppeteers instigating their jerky *danse macabre*.

No such fires for us in this modern age. At six in the morning our thermostat judges the rooms too cold and switches on the central heating with a WHOOSH! so that, by the time I rise half an hour later, the house is snug, a cocoon against the frosty bite of reality outside. Somewhat hypocritically though, despite loving the warm convenience of the radiators, I'm very thankful during the walk to work to find that more than one elderly neighbour remains staunchly politically incorrect, meaning that, for at least one more year, my frosty autumn mornings will be laced with that lovely, homely tang of coal smoke.

This was not a time for cool contemplation, for formal remembrance and distant memories. This would have been time to split the air and earth wide open, to tease the borders of the world into liminal pick-holes through which the dead could slip and the fairies could dance and those loved ones departed could stride openly across their remembered landscapes, visiting their former homes for one more night to take up the places set for them by their families.

Here, too, come my ghosts. Here come those men who have shared my nights and my tides. Always foremost amongst them, my grandfather, his stocky outline casting its huge, comforting shadow over the ground and everything else, but behind him step three more: the uncles. Here are the brothers, his sons, Paul and Lyndon. Where one mimicked my grandfather's shape and quick humour, the other was his polar opposite.: tall, serious; the pious lay preacher whose sharp humour could still glint like a blade when unsheathed. Both lost to illness, both before the age of forty-five. I had shared tides with them both.

From behind them steps the third, Chris, the baby, my mother's brother, younger by a few years than I am now when his demons caught up with him and claimed him for their own. For today they have returned him to me, his lifeboat crewman's swaggering confidence around the sea, his quick chatter, easy smile, constant joking and ability to spot a bite where others saw none.

And now, one last presence makes itself known, the largest of them all – big Andy. With my grandfather's build and a six-foot two-inch frame, this no-nonsense Lancastrian was the second of the two great pillars of my early fishing years.

I hadn't been sea fishing for long when this giant of a man began to turn up at the places in which I was loitering with my grandfather. When we fished the breakwater this man was there; when we fished the surf for bass he seemed to be there too. Then I started to see him strolling through the town centre, then the local corner shop and, finally, passing my living room window.

Then one day, my grandfather, who could talk a glass eye to sleep underwater, approached him and struck up a conversation. I feigned interest in the static rod tips for five minutes then wandered over myself, and the rest is history.

After discovering that he had and his family had moved in just two doors down, from then on my Fridays would be punctuated with the heavy tones of "Y' coomin' fishin' temorra lad?" Temorra could never come around quick enough, especially if the session was in the early hours of the morning. If we were to set out for one (our street was ten minutes' walk from the beach) I would be at his house for ten to partake of endless brews that had stewed to the colour of treacle, and cadged cigarettes before, the world finally put to rights, he roused to gather his gear together.

My classroom door opens a chink, then big Andy is gone again for another year, disappearing as the door is flung wide and a chattering turmoil of kids pours into the room ready for the next lesson.

"What are you looking at, sir?" they ask. I tell them as they take their seats, tell them about all of it: conkers; seasons; lost friends; fishing. Sometimes I like to forestall the business of learning and tell a story or two before pressing on; always the angler, ready with a tale.

"Really, sir? You go fishing? Why?!" The reaction of my students is always the same. I can't generalise and buy into the adage that *kids nowadays ain't what they used to be*. When I look out across the faces in front of me and see the expressions of some of those kids, pasty, with bags under the eyes, I recognise in them the same tiredness I wore the morning after a late midweek session (when I could get away with it), only their tiredness and pasty complexion come more from being cooped up in their bedrooms, playing out some action scene in a virtual world far removed from reality.

Whether they're grossed out by the idea of handling worms and fish, whether the concept of spending time in the outdoors is alien to them or whether the thought of catching fish is simply too primal and ancient for their modern sensibilities, I don't know.

What I do know is that these days, as the seasons pass, I'm less often surrounded by young faces on the beaches. There is far more to compete with these days for those of us who often stand out in the elements, our cold hands knuckling around the rod, casting a quick glance back at the rig hanging from a line behind us before turning, ready to smack it as hard as we can, and to hope for a little longer.

"Right then," I say. "Bags on the floor; books open. It's time to move on."

V – At the Year's Closing

At This Time of the Rolling Year

"Com on wanre niht scriðan sceadugenga"

- Beowulf

Finally, the classroom is quiet. The autumn term is the busiest term at school and this one has been no different – new arrivals, new schemes of work, the season of parents' evenings and meetings; but now, after sixteen long weeks, it has come to an end. Ten minutes ago my last class of the term, a rowdy year nine group, bolted screaming through the doors leaving a trail of disturbed chairs and sweet wrappers drifting back down to earth. But I'm in no rush to follow them despite it being only a few days from Christmas Eve.

The last day of term is always a time of quiet reflection, but the autumn term even more so with its shorter days, the town settling into its long winter slumber. I clear my desk, wipe the board clean and finish off the last of my cup of tea as the battery charger on the left of my desk blinks green. All day I have been charging the sets of batteries in readiness and now that the last of them is ready, I pack the last of my things into my satchel and leave the classroom, locking the door behind me.

It is only just after four o' clock, but already the moon is risen, its gunshot outline bleeding the streets of their colour in the last of their watery lymph- light.

Leaving through the front doors, I notice that the car park is already all but empty, except for the light still blazing in the Head's office just to the left of the doors – the Captain is refusing to abandon his ship just yet, steering it through the last moments of the term.

A stand of bare sycamores stands off to my right, held up against the darkening sky where a breeze begins its work. The space between the scrawny limbs seems to expand and quiver as though sucking in a deep racking breath of air that has finally cleared now that all the leafy sediment of autumn has settled.

From the shadows of these branches a corvid creak seems to

open the door to the fast-arriving darkness.

Winter is here.

During summer's embarrassment of riches, it's easy to lose yourself in plain sight – those seemingly endless days of bright sunshine and everlasting blue skies a massive expanse into which you can slip and vanish. Winter, though, has the opposite effect – everything shrinks back, draws in, reducing the world to a series of little vignettes: the walk home becomes a series of exposed, lamp lit staging posts, lurching from one pool of light to the next, putting things into sharp perspective as you walk on. It frames us – glancing up occasionally, we see individuals beavering away in silhouette behind the drawn blinds of their office windows, little shadow-puppet shows acted out in isolation behind the frosted windows, the early nights and floodlit evening sports games all happening in isolation from one another in these villages of light.

This is a world of sharp, juxtaposed contrasts – the abundance of the Christmas displays shining out on a world that has a distinctly thrifty appearance.

*

Less than three hours later and I'm beavering away in the dark, zipping in and out through the shed's light, back and forth, packing the car ready for the long session to come: rods, floatation suit, box containing the reels, terminal tackle and two flasks – one of coffee and one of vegetable soup. The boot closes with a clunk that teeters on the hollow acoustics of asphalt and concrete, then dissipates. The final kisses goodbye are given and I step through the front door, cutting off the warm stream of light and locking up for the night behind me.

Before I start out, I must choose music for the journey which, at this time of year, often means choral music. Each note is perfected within its own structure, a snowflake of sound and, as always, I am unable to stop the mental association I immediately make between the unfolding song and the forming of hoar frost, its hollow tubes reaching out, building upon themselves. But what to go with? Maybe start with something like Holst's *In the Bleak Midwinter*, or possibly a bit of Lauridsen's O Magnum Mysterium.

Perhaps a little more appropriate to this particular night would be Rachmaninov's *All-Night Vigil*, with its tonal, coloured Eastern Orthodox sound-tapestry. Yes, I think *All-Night Vigil* would be good now, particularly section four: *Joyful Light*, perhaps because the composer wrote it in the earliest, coldest months of the year, or maybe because of the natural tone of lamentation carried by the music. For whatever reason it just feels an apt fit for the season, the lament of the tenor chorus that seems to bemoan the slipping of the year into its senescent months interlocking neatly to the very first notes of the sopranos, reaching up and up in supplication, the notes chiming one upon another. Then that lone tenor voice breaks from the crowd and begins to plead, dragging the soprano voices back up to a crescendo, the urgency of the voices building as that frost begins to crisp the land outside the church door.

As those Baltic temperatures begin to plummet further, the voices of those northern faithful start to diminish and mesh and turn inward once more, but not before a final flourish, a last act of contrition begging the Lord to stay with them, to sustain them through the long, hard winter to come and see them through to the other side as the movement begins to close down, the deep arctic darkness taking hold, the singers peering out for one final time before the huge wooden doors groan closed with the low ache of the basso profundo voices that rumble down and down through the octaves, a final vocal genuflection before the bar drops into place with a muffled thud.

The car starts first time, the lights flick on, slitting a pocket open in the winter evening; I put the car into first gear and slip into the ink-silky blackness.

The drive is short and over in minutes when I park the car and stop to watch for a moment as the wraiths of heat and exhaust fumes wind their wispy undulations through the probing beams of the headlight. There is much room for the music to spread as I open the car window to allow in a bracing blast of freezing air, and the song tinkles out to strike against the emptying evening like a tuning fork before I flick the engine off and begin to unpack.

There is, I think, something of a pioneer air about anyone who ventures out on such nights. Looking about me as I pull on my boots, I can see the world of other people divided neatly into lamp-lit parcels of happiness complete with crossed ribbon window frames, glowing exaggeratedly like those yellow-paned cardboard churches we all drew on our handmade cards at Primary school.

My mind begins to wander as I lace up the boots, and I begin to imagine what's going on behind those panes, a strange melding of the great story from ancient Judea, the traditions of Victorian Britain and a little of the prosperous glitz of 1950's America. Maybe trees are being decorated, families are starting to tuck into the Christmas chocs and breaking open the first case of festive wine, laughing to the throb of Slade and Wizard, wheeling out those old festive clichés that we all know and mock and secretly cherish as a guilty pleasure. Maybe presents are even being wrapped. But whatever they may be doing, to all of them I do not even exist out here; I might as well be sat amongst the freezing remoteness of a distant planet's rings.

In contemplating the spring, Wordsworth commented on "that sweet mood when pleasant thoughts/Bring sad thoughts to the mind", highlighting the natural balance that must always occur between good and bad. The negative must exist if only to counterbalance the positive and make us appreciate it for what it is. These people, though, seem to have forgotten that such a balance can, and should, exist. Their lights blare out, pushing the dark away from their windowpanes, allowing the rest of the world to look in upon all the wonders their lives contain, but prevent them from seeing out and acknowledging that the dark exists, the reflections of their own lives bouncing back at them from the inside of the glass so that all they can see is a transposed interpretation of themselves, baubles and tinsel and all.

Ready now, I turn to take in the pier itself. The site of industry, life and action that buzzed through the summer months has long since gone. All that made it alive has departed, leaving behind a long, grey slab of concrete, a huge catafalque lying solid and sombre out in the bay. A classic whiting night means that there is little tide, leaving only the silence of the altar and the random lights of those who have already arrived before me to begin their night's long vigil.

Rather than feeling desolate and lonely on such a place in the depths of winter, I feel that I can better understand how those remote monasteries like Lindisfarne were founded where they were, as here the same remoteness, silence, power and, often, awe, are palpable. There is a world of difference between loneliness and solitude and this place epitomises it succinctly in its frost-covered surface, stretching out like silver desert sands.

Of his time at the Abbey of St. Wandrille, after going in search of a tranquillity all his own, Patrick Leigh Fermor wrote that 'time passes in a monastery with disconcerting speed…there are no landmarks to divide it up except the cycle of seasons…six months, a year, fifteen years, a lifetime, are soon over.' Of course, it would take the eyes of an outsider to see it in such a way, for time as we know it – the twenty-four-hour day; the seven-day week; does not exist or, at the very least, holds no relevance for those whose eyes are ever fixed upon the eternal.

Outside, in a functional, modern world that is increasingly ruled by 'the unforgiving minute', we must, if we are to begin comprehending anything within a sense of scale, consider the world in weeks and months and years, but part of the attraction of fishing these places at these times of year, is the fact that the light is gone by around four o clock and we are left with a synthetic version of monasticism, sealed into separateness by the dark and the silence, each angler standing, waiting, as though caught out by a quickly retreating ebb tide, waiting and investing their faith in the long darkness not measured by seconds and minutes and hours but by the slow pulse of the tides and the surges of fish periodically carried by them through our lives.

The journey to the fishing spot is short but cluttered by the accumulated bits and pieces racked up throughout the year – that boulder, there, where I caught that four-pound bass back when summer was in full swing; just on the beach beneath me, across an area now somewhere beneath a dozen feet of water, I winkled out a few crabs for a smooth hound session.

Fishing-wise, these rocks seem to encompass everything for me – they are yesterday, today and tomorrow, the place where I cut my teeth, having spent time here with my father, uncles and both grandfathers, the place where I regularly fish now whenever I get a chance, where my own daughter was trundled down in a buggy as I fished for rays, and the place where others will continue to fish after I am gone. It seems immoveable, a rock rampart that puts its shoulder to every tide, ready to defeat, to defend, but even these stones, I know, won't last.

Breakwater

Twice each day, the sea takes
what might be the final glance
at all it will outlast.

September spring tides
and the winter storms
resonate with deep, muffled thuds;
beneath the surface those boulders
grind and collide, awkward
in confronting the bare fact
that we can never *break* water,
only turn it aside.

But while they are still here, and while I am here to fish them, I continue along the short route that I could walk in my sleep, across a flat concrete platform and down, down over a slope of boulders, just one part of the sea defences placed along the length of the beach years ago, that leads to the ragged concrete surface of the breakwater. Before the introduction of the boulder slopes, there was simply a set of concrete steps that led down onto the beach itself. They looked nothing ordinary, but at high tide, when the water reached them, they looked like the entrance to some Tír na nÓg of the imagination. Every summer we would come here on the highest tides and wait for the waves to help with the deliveries from this other world, watching on as the swell heaved and shunted the silvered treasures of whitebait, scad, mackerel, occasional garfish and, if we were very lucky, the bass that were hunting them all, up onto the steps where we would race down between the backwash and the next wave to claim our prizes. Those days are gone now, the steps covered beneath feet of rock, but there lingers a strange feeling that this is a place of passage and of mutability.

Passing the canopic glowering of a lone gull and heading out onto the breakwater itself, I arrive at my chosen spot. To begin with, I feel completely alone despite the scant lights of a couple of others, so I quickly set about the deliberate placement of a base camp. The tripod is set up and rods and reels quickly placed in their notches – one rigged up with a simple flapping Wessex rig that will be cast only ten yards from the outer edge of the rocks, the other with a two hook clipped down rig that will be sent out like a tendril, scouting the sand between 50 and 100 yards out. The petrol lamp is lifted from the bucket, lighted and the whole backdrop is illuminated. A sudden flitting as something alters its trajectory of flight through the lamp's unexpected pocket of light, the moth dipping and rising and weaving, its trail a faint flicker of a pulse. The small perimeter of brightness seems scant comfort, but the little heat it offers will be enough to warm the hands from time to time and stop the lugworms from freezing in the sub-zero temperatures. Hanging it from the tripod's bucket hook allows it to throw out maximum light, but as I bustle around it my shadow is cast and magnified onto the shortarm – a larger breakwater further along the beach, stooping, crouching, then springing up malevolently as it mimics and mocks my every movement.

I scan the other anglers to see if I recognise anyone else. I've seen the guy nearest to me before – I call him Mister Red Mist, for two main reasons. For one thing, everything about him is red, from his floatation suit to his rod and his reel. He could almost be mistaken for Father Christmas, particularly at this time of year, were it not for reason two – the fact that he tends to use the word "fuck" as a form of punctuation, which in turn gives his face a lingering angry expression that seems totally at odds with his gently sibilant nickname. I can still recall our last conversation some nine or ten months ago going something like

"Caught much?"

"Fuck all, mate. Not fuckin' bitin' at the moment and I've thrown every fuckin' thing at 'em. Brought some lug – big fuckers an' all – some squid and some mackerel that absolutely fuckin' stinks, but the fuckers are havin' none of it. Fuck me, I'm bored."

For now, I shall take the colour red at its traffic sign values and give him a bit of a wide berth.

The only other angler, thirty yards further along, checks his phone. Its screen casts a weak blue tint that is not enough to illuminate his body but its 'dismal light' is enough to make him look like Scrooge's first glimpse of Marley's ghost from this distance.

"*What do you want with me?*" Scrooge asked Marley in Dickens' tale.

"*Much!*" came the reply, and in a similar vein, there is much that this season has had to do with me. As the ghosts urged Scrooge to do, I sit and reflect for a minute, particularly on the impact that winter has had on my life and come to realise that the season holds many of my most significant experiences.

When very young, I would spend most weekends at my grandparents' house, the most distinct bonus of which, for a young boy, was the fact that my grandfather was a building site foreman and would more often than not take me to work with him on a Saturday morning. The men on that site took me under their wing, offering a totally different kind of education and introducing me, at the age of nine, to such joys as strong coffee, and teaching me how to drive a forklift truck, so that many weekends saw me crunching those big tyres across the frost-hard mudscape of the site with a half-mug of Nescafe sloshing around in my hand.

It was also through these men that I learned the joys of the female form and of poetry, both, strangely enough, at the same time. Although I had access to the key of the managerial portaloo, its pristine, bland convenience wasn't half as interesting as the graffitied wisdom on the walls of the portaloo used by the other men. My grandfather didn't particularly like my using it, but when he was busy somewhere around the site, I spent hours shivering in there gazing up at the eye-boggling spread-eagled cut-outs from magazines of a less-than-salubrious nature, and reading its earthy wisdoms etched in blue biro, including many instances of what happens to nuns when they walk into bars, such philosophical gems as "*I shit, therefore I stink*", and one of the first poems I ever learned by rote:

> Here I sit
> Broken-hearted,
> Tried to shit
> But only farted.

There are so many other things that spring to mind, such as my first cider-tainted kiss in a dilapidated, waterlogged old adventure playground that had frozen into iron and ice-rink puddles one freezing December afternoon; those Christmas parties at relatives' houses that would see my family rambling back home through the streets in the early hours, the empty streets echoing flintily; and then there is, of course, that first experience of night fishing.

No ghosts may visit me tonight, but all these thoughts of the past, along with many others, will appear and disappear as the hours pass.

The baits are laid out on the lid of the bucket – although I've brought them, there really is not much need for more expensive worm and crab baits tonight; the fish here will be plentiful and hungry so fish, prawn and shellfish will more than suffice.

The foreknowledge of what can be caught here at this time is no black magic, but it does almost allow an angler a brief glimpse into the future and the opportunity to be prepared. When the voracious winter shoals of whiting, pout and dabs come on the feed there is no time to leisurely cut bait if the opportunity is to be maximised. As such, little tubs of mackerel chunks and sprat fillets are stacked like currency, ready to buy my way into the night. I know of at least a few anglers who refuse to wet a line until they have made an offering to the sea in the form of a silver coin, and now here I am, so near to Christ's Mass and the celebration of His birth, ready to make my own offerings to some older powers, casting little flickering silver offerings into the black waters.

The first baits are soon in the water – small chunks of fish impaled on size 1 fine-wire hooks tethered to snoods of no more than eight inches in length – when contact is made I want it to be certain. Even though from half tide onward I know the fish will be coming, there is still an element of impatient but peaceful waiting for that first bite which seems wholly appropriate to the season of

Advent.

The tide is high tonight, and already it's pushing up toward the pitted concrete surface of the pier. The gentlest of swells lazily heaves itself past my position, lifting and then lowering the reflections of the stars for a moment before they settle again within my field of vision like ducks upon a rock-shattered pond. In an hour this whole area will be partially submerged, meaning that we will all be in a liminal zone somewhere between dry land and submersion. The scarified old concrete surface has weathered out hundreds of storms and bears the marks in the weed-hung "rock pools" that pit the surface all the way down the breakwater's length. The tides over the years have done their best to hollow out the space beneath my feet and now the rising tide forces air around in a hissing, gurgling broth of air and seawater.

The first isn't long in coming, though it's not to my rod. Further up toward the breakwater's end there is a shout and a white flexing flash zips through a circle of light, a dogfish, most likely, judging by the size and shape, closely followed by a body stumbling down from the rocks. The body's companions close in, a shadow at a time, to take a quick look at the fish before receding again, and the fish is quickly released back over the side, a short incomplete arc of white that disappears from sight before it reaches the water.

As I watch the goings-on further along, a sharp movement from the corner of my eye catches my attention, forcing my head to involuntarily swing around just as the last vibrations tremble from the tip of the rod fishing nearest the rocks. A breathless moment; always this breathless moment. Many wouldn't even bother to sneer down their nose at what I'm guessing this might be, but the whiting truly is my favourite fish, so representative of my first nights spent so far from the comforts of bed and home.

After spending so much of my early years tucked away from the night-time realities of the big wide world, my earliest night sessions seemed incursions into some other existence altogether, an existence where the town was amazingly quiet and still; the cool night air even smelt different to the daytime air. This was all about going beneath the surface, about living by a different set of senses in a shamanic dream world where time seemed to melt away and murmurations of whiting passed through like starlings. And so the humble whiting become attached, a kind of spirit-animal, to my nocturnal consciousness and all my after-dark ramblings.

Still I wait. Could I have imagined it? The human eye is so unreliable, especially in such poor light. No, no mistake; here it is again, a positive rattle.

Quickly, I lift the rod from the stand and my light tentatively pokes out over the water in front of me, scanning for whatever breaks the surface. A double shot of a whiting and a dab breaks surface only ten yards out and flutters into my circle, safely claimed. It is only a small job to unhook them and slip them back - too small, or these delicious little fish would be coming back for the pan.

Deeper into the small hours we descend, the temperature plummeting, the air cut to pieces on the keen edge of an easterly wind. Our lights burn on, though now, in the freezing cold small hours, they don't seem so solid and certain, as the flecks of rain so cold that they seem to steam, corroding and pitting the headlamp beams like the surface of old iron pipes.

Still, none of us has drifted homeward yet. For hours now, people and fish have flashed in and out of the light and we have all watched from our own little colonised patches, catching these glimpses of other lives playing out, their busyness, testing energy, bait supplies and enthusiasm almost to their limit. And still, over the top of the tide and into the beginnings of the ebb they come – whiting; pouting; codling; dogfish; dab; all reduced to white flickers in the lights, passing through and then into darkness again like little phantoms.

None of us can leave: we are haunted men; haunted by these little visitors, haunted by the year growing ever older, haunted by the knowledge that, although we can, theoretically, pack in and re-join the real world at any time, winter will still be there waiting for us in its iron-hard, year-spanning persistence.

The rain stopped over an hour ago as the temperature completely dropped out of the night, but now my final session of the year seems set to end in the way that the first one of the year began – the snow has arrived again. It's nothing like as heavy as that first snow, but enough to show up in the headlamps and provide a short distraction from the insatiable shoals.

It's light enough at the moment to watch individual flakes fall until they disappear, dissolved into the wetness of the pier's surface or evaporating with a tiny hiss the second they hit the hot pressure lantern. The image of snow rings a bell in my head, and for a second I am too tired to make the link that my brain is trying to force upon me until it finally clicks. I spent half an hour a few days ago, reading about a man called Wilson Bentley, or 'The Snowflake Man' as he later became known. By chilling a tray of velvet, he was able to capture snowflakes without their melting then, through long years of basic but meticulous photography and scraping, managing to prove that every snowflake is individual while, in the process, collating a catalogue containing thousands of some of the most wonderfully illuminating images of snowflakes that are still fresh and beautifully intricate now, over a hundred years after they were produced. The man who made microscopic milliseconds last a lifetime.

If Wilson Bentley managed to work with such patience and diligence, harvesting a lifetime's worth of moments, I can certainly manage awhile longer, snow or no snow. So, it seems that there is nothing else to do; I shall fish on through the ebb and the darkness and all the snow's little epiphanies, casting blindly toward a dawn that still seems so very far away.

A Trillion Blooms

Wilson "Snowflake" Bentley

Homespun wisdom ready
to weave back into the edge
of some blossoming storm,
You waited on,
anticipating such spirit-harvests
springing from their own short seasons.

In imagination
or deep in long-held memory,
each tiny flake was already a window.

I see you, or maybe just think I do,
still looking through onto some dream meadow,
a trillion faceted blooms,
flickering in
a building breeze.

Editorials

The mug steams away on the sill at my left hand, a book on the table to my right. The candle flickers atop the bookshelf, making a little island in the shadows and offering just enough light to read by. I settle deep into silence, unbroken except for the soft creaking feedback of my battered leather armchair taking up the slack.

This house, arthritic centurion, is both old enough and wise enough to tolerate me, or perhaps even too old to care about my presence, telling a story through all those tics and groans, the weight and experience of a dozen lives lived here before me, a hundred and fifteen winters weathered out; from the most recent inhabitants before us, through the steelworker Alfred Ferris back in the sixties, through a period of ownership by the Church in Wales right back to the earliest owners: Rhys Hopkins, collier, Thomas Evans, builder, and the tin worker David Evans over a hundred years ago, whose signature appears alongside that of Emily Charlotte Talbot, last of the Talbot family bearing that name to live in the great house that is Margam Castle.

Like some fable figure, it arrives out of all these lives and its own years into this evening, an Urashima or Oisin, to find itself suddenly so old and the world around it completely altered: the introduction of cars, the invention and installation of television aerials and even indoor toilets have all come to pass in its lifetime, so now it too settles back in quietly, safe in the knowledge that it will certainly outlast me, and probably my grandchildren.

Another squall bursts handfuls of gravel-rain upon the window, tittering like a child that runs away before hurling another handful over its shoulder and I sink back even deeper, slightly smug at my decision to leave the rods stacked away in the shed tonight. Unlike those ancient legends, I haven't managed to escape the world for three hundred years, but it does suddenly seem as though a year's worth of fishing has passed in the blink of an eye.

Tonight was meant to be my last session of the year, a chance for one or two final codling, but it is no night for fishing. After the lights of Christmas, we have slunk back into winter rain; from glory to greyness. Driving back from Swansea in the darkness earlier, the motorway lights, through the prismatic effects of the rain upon the rain-spattered window, wore a pale nimbus, each individual light appearing to sway like luminous dandelion heads ready to be blown away into the evening. Such is fishing: where earlier the evening had carried hopes and ideas of great fish, these last days of the year have begun to circle around, and it has now become a night for dreaming about fishing and fishes and other things that have been and gone, both those from the last twelve months and those long since blown away like dandelions themselves.

No doubt, these dreams will come quickly when I fall asleep halfway through the next chapter, as per usual. They'll rise from all depths - the recently caught and lost, the wished-for and unfished-for; and maybe they'll come up from far deeper. Occasionally, memory sends up my first ever fish – a rudd. Four ounces of molten loveliness, it had swiped a maggot from under a quill one balmy evening after school and dragged it out of sight and now, shaped and polished by all the years of fond mental handling, there's no other fish that can ever come close to comparing to it.

Or maybe I'll revisit that day on the pontoon. A shoal of rudd had flicked into a feeding frenzy as I shredded a stale loaf of Hovis over the water. Then, from a ball of writhing activity, they fluttered away like confetti and I was left with nothing but a great green-grey snake of an eel that insinuated itself to the surface, looked me over with a withering glance that seemed to hold pure disdain for my having caused all the commotion, before it slid back down out of sight to its lair in the pilings.

Nothing remarkable, and nothing any coarse angler hasn't seen a thousand times, but as soon as that sight came in through the eyes and entered my head, that was it. In that second, the process began: the mental editor went to work, crafting, remoulding, refining everything down and trimming off all the unnecessary details.

All angling stories will meander along different paths, whether they tell of coastal storms, weed-covered rocks and darkest coastline outposts, the meticulous, ordered efficacy of an arduous coarse match win or the romanticised panache of the nomad, drifting along miles of some fast-flowing stream flicking a fly for hard-hitting trout, but when all is said and done, fish are fish and all our pitches and piers and banksides are just that – places where we caught a few during a quiet couple of hours.

But when they are submitted to that dark little office between the ears, that's when everything changes. This is what happens when the Editor takes over. The Editor doesn't care about truth in the strictest sense, he just wants a nice, neat, appealing version of events. "***For God's sake, entertain the audience!***" he screams from way back there in your head; "***Give 'em the good bits!***" So you do, stretching, squeezing, comparing, smoothing over and, (whisper it), exaggerating. All those broken reel handles, miscasts, crack-offs have no longer happened; that bait isn't left behind in your fridge, but has somehow appeared, as if by magic, in your bucket; those dogs that ate the bait or peed on the tackle have trotted off to their owners leaving you alone with a knowing little grin and some very happy memories.

So, even though I can vividly recall that first little fish, I can't remember my first blank session. Try as I might, I can't, for the life of me, recall any of it. Where was I? What was I fishing for? What was the bait? The weather? The tackle? Beats me. That's all gone now, sitting coiled up and ignored on some mental cutting-room floor or scrumpled in a basket with a thick black line through it.

On nights like tonight, such realities have no place.

And then, when they've been subjected to the close scrutiny of the Editor, these memories become something else. Sculpted, developed, honed – they have become more like artefacts now, things that are complete and independent from us, so that we no longer have any control over what happens to them. And like archaeological artefacts, they tell their own story now and have to be understood apart from a context that has long since vanished. Come back in a week and find a little less rain; come back in a month and there may be an extra fish; come back in a couple of years and it was a red-letter day. They constantly evolve and surprise us and go on in an ever changing process of renewal and renovation and become much like these books I'm surrounded by now: an archive of the lovely, the pleasurable and the felt-by-heart, all well-thumbed, all with an uncanny sense of something you've experienced before but can't quite put your finger on.

Time moves on and takes with it much of memory. The beginnings of our years are always full of 'Go' and see us keen to break from the anchorage of the old year and press on into the new. Whether it's the challenge of the unknown, or the temptation of heading into the untainted, like stepping onto virgin snow, all those year openings seem pregnant with the possibility for redemption in their new beginnings. But of course, the years speed up, and begin to leave us behind, so often causing us to race toward the back ends of those years in a manner that seems far beyond all our control, and so we tend to lean a little more back toward nostalgia. We turn instead to what we remember, relying upon it to act as a drogue, slowing us down a little, forcing us to ease off the pedal, allowing life to catch up with us, or, perhaps more accurately, enabling us to catch up with life.

I break from my daydream for a minute and pick up the book again: *The Great Gatsby*, my favourite novel, realising that I have arrived at the last page once more. Every year I read this book and every year I understand it in a slightly different way, seeing Gatsby as weak and arrogant and child-like in turn, but always, the ending reads the same.

I read the final sentences again, thinking of how we all have our own green light, our own gas-lit bivvy or chemical tip light or headlamp beam that leads us on beyond some simplistic longing for the past, causing us to dip into memory until those things we recall and think about and obsess about and dream about while we struggle against the currents of time, begin to form the excitements of our today and lay down the building blocks of our tomorrow.

There will, no doubt, be even more work for the Editor in the new year to come; more real life and ugly truth to pore over and excise, but for now, he and I have a cup of tea, a storm to wait out, a stack of books and time enough to ponder back over one or two more of the old favourites before it will be time to call it a night.

Acknowledgements

Acknowledgements are due to the following publications and sites in which some of these pieces, or sections of them, first appeared:

- Countryman magazine
- Creative Countryside
- Fallon's Angler
- Waterlog
- Welsh Country
- www.naturewriting.com

Citations

Page 28 - "...the snow falling faintly through the universe and faintly falling, like the descent of their last end." - James Joyce, *The Dead* taken from Dubliners, (1914)

Page 33 - "Sea sounds were the concomitant of Celtic prayer. Without sea-cadence, prayer to them sounded thin." – Ronald Blythe, *Cedd's Essex Adventure*, taken from River Diary, published by Canterbury Press (Canterbury Press Norwich, 13-17 Long Lane, London, EC1A 9PN) (2008)

Page 131 – "...time passes in a monastery with disconcerting speed...there are no landmarks to divide it up except the cycle of seasons...six months, a year, fifteen years, a lifetime, are soon over.." – Patrick Leigh Fermor, *A Time To Keep Silence*, John Murray (John Murray, 50 Albemarle St, London W15 4BD) (2004)

www.ingramcontent.com/pod-product-compliance
Lightning Source LLC
Chambersburg PA
CBHW061658040426
42446CB00010B/1792